Scottish by Inclination

To Marybel,

BARBARA HENDERSON

Choose to belong!

Barbara Henderson

Luath Press Limited

EDINBURGH

www.luath.co.uk

First published 2021

ISBN: 978-1-910022-42-9

The paper used in this book is recyclable.
It is made from low chlorine pulps
produced in a low energy, low emission manner
from renewable forests.

Barbara Henderson acknowledges support from the National Lottery
through Creative Scotland towards the writing of this title.

Printed and bound by
Bell & Bain Ltd, Glasgow

Typeset in 11 point Sabon by
Main Point Books, Edinburgh

BARBARA HENDERSON is an Inverness-based children's writer and Drama teacher. Her energetic school visits take her across the length and breadth of Scotland, and sometimes beyond. As a teacher, she loves to get young people on their feet as they respond to stories. 'Writing is like magic,' she says. 'I see something in my imagination, and I try to capture it by writing it down – nothing more than black marks on white paper. Much later, young people see these black marks on white paper and suddenly they see something too, feel something of their own. I cannot think of anything more special than that.' *Scottish by Inclination* is Barbara's first foray into adult non-fiction. She shares her home with her teenage son, her long-suffering husband and a scruffy Schnauzer called Merry.

Praise for *Scottish by Inclination*

Scottish by Inclination *is a revealing snapshot of a moment in history: the Brexit referendum and its implementation. In it, Barbara Henderson, who has made Scotland her home since 1991, focuses on thirty individual, moving, funny, heartening or troubling perspectives on what it is, or was, to be a newcomer, or immigrant, to Scotland, from one of the other member states of the EU.* PROFESSOR DAVID WORTHINGTON

Without Brexit, Scottish By Inclination *might not have been written – and whatever you think of the 2016 vote, that would be a huge shame. In this affectionate and warm-hearted look at what it means to be a 'new Scot' in 2021, German-born teacher and author Barbara Henderson talks to a range of EU nationals living and working in Scotland. Inevitably, the shadow of the 2016 vote falls over their experiences, but on reading Barbara's book, it's impossible not to feel humbled that so many talented and resourceful people from across Europe have chosen to make Scotland their home. One only hopes that her optimistic conclusion that 'we're going to be okay' comes true.* MARGARET KIRK, award-winning author of *Shadow Man*

A wonderful compendium of voices, as varied as the continent of Europe itself, Barbara's Scottish by Inclination *gives us what often seems lacking in these dark times – optimism and celebration of our shared future.'* DONALD S. MURRAY, author of *As the Women Lay Dreaming*

By the same author:

Fir for Luck, Cranachan Publishing, 2016
Punch, Cranachan Publishing, 2017
Wilderness Wars, Cranachan Publishing, 2018
Black Water, Cranachan Publishing, 2019
The Siege of Caerlaverock, Cranachan Publishing, 2020
The Chessmen Thief, Cranachan Publishing, 2021

Contents

To all the Scots, by birth or by inclination,
who have made Scotland home for me.

Forgetting I Was a Foreigner

No borders, just horizons, only freedom. – Amelia Earhart

SEVERAL YEARS AGO, I heard a politician use the phrase 'Scottish by inclination' on the news.

I sat up. 'Wait, what did he just say?'

My husband shrugged. 'Scottish by inclination.'

'You can be Scottish by inclination? As in, if you want to be in, you're in?'

'I think that's what he means, yeah.'

The conversation may have been over, but the expression stayed with me. *Scottish by inclination.* If you feel inclined to be Scottish, you can be. End of story. There was something open-armed about the phrase and I loved it. It stirred something in me, though I couldn't put my finger on it.

Years later, I had another chance encounter with the phrase. I was browsing through opportunities for unpublished writers, and there it was again: a publication invited work from 'writers resident in Scotland or Scots by birth, upbringing or inclination'.

I felt the same pang of longing.

As a German national who came to Edinburgh to study in 1991 and never left, the expression resonated strongly with me. I think I am not alone in finding the immigrant status unsettling, at least in terms of identity. For the majority of my three decades here, my birth country did not allow dual nationality. In other words, I would have had to give up my German nationality in order to become British, while I had ageing parents living on the continent. I decided against pursuing a British passport. It would have felt like denying my heritage. And after all, there was no need to – I had the right to live and work in the UK and move freely around the European Union.

Back in 1991, there was widespread optimism about European collaborations in many fields, including academia. The EU had just offered to cover whole-degree tuition fees, removing the key obstacle to my ambition to study abroad. I yearned to experience another culture and to improve my English, so applying to a fistful of reputable Scottish universities simply made sense.

Edinburgh's thriving international student community offered me support in practical terms and friends from all corners of the world. I found the Scots welcoming and open-minded – so much so that I married one of them.

And so the course for my permanent residence in Scotland was set. My husband was training to be a doctor. Were we to settle in Germany, his command of the language would have had to be near perfect to practise medicine safely, aside from the extra qualifications he'd have to obtain. I, on the other hand, had graduated here in Scotland, and was able to progress on my career path unhindered. Staying was logical, the sensible option. Gradually, with a Scottish husband and three Scottish children, I forgot I was a foreigner.

Fast forward almost three decades, and the rhetoric in public discourse had shifted significantly. Some of the headlines in the run-up to the 2016 referendum on Britain's EU membership, for example, made my skin crawl. Anti-immigrant views were publicly aired once more, and even people I considered friends (and still do!) voted to leave in order to 'take back control'.

When I was honest about my fears, they protested quickly. 'We don't mean *you*, obviously. It's not about *you*, or people like you.' I nodded, pretending to understand.

If they didn't mean me, who on earth were they referring to? People who did not speak good English yet? People who needed help? People who, for the sake of family, or poverty, or education, had the audacity to wish for a better life?

The political climate made me defensive. I found myself telling strangers that I had never lived off benefits and had worked and paid tax ever since my graduation in the mid-'90s. That I was a teacher in the Highlands, an area where recruitment and retention of qualified education staff is often challenging. That I initiated a book festival in my home city of Inverness and served as chairperson for several years. It was all true. Come to think of it, there hasn't been a single year in my three decades in Scotland in which I have not volunteered regularly in some way: as a school librarian, on the school PTA, running free classes at a local theatre, in church, with the elderly, in the arts, in conservation. My six novels for children are widely studied in Scottish primary classrooms. I travel the country to visit schools and promote a love of reading and of Scottish cultural heritage. If I am honest, I wanted these strangers to know that I was worth having, here in Scotland.

I am not unique. Many EU citizens who have made their home here have become integral to their communities, succeeded and even excelled in their chosen fields, created community initiatives, filled much-needed vacancies and brought with them an international outlook which our country needs to hold on to. They are Scottish by inclination, just as I am. I felt uncertainty on behalf of us all, and a little indignation too.

I am a writer – words are my way of wrestling with the world. Could I make the case for the enrichment of EU immigration in a book? I pitched the idea in a tweet: 'Scottish by Inclination. Activists, academics, artists, radiologists and removal men. A chapter-by-chapter collection of interesting stories of EU nationals who have made their homes here and are helping to shape what Scotland is today.'

'We like the concept,' Gavin MacDougall of Luath Press said. 'But have you thought of adding a personal dimension to the book? Telling your own story?'

I declined immediately. 'No, I don't think so. That wasn't what I had in mind.'

But the more I reflected, the more I felt I had to say. I attempted a trial chapter and discovered that I was simply processing the concerns and cares which were already at the forefront of my mind. Writing my part, I'm willing to admit, felt a little cathartic.

I got back in touch with the publisher. 'If you're still interested, I think I'm going to give it a go after all.'

Thirty interviews, a funding application and many writing hours later, I'm glad I did, because all voices matter and deserve to belong.

Belonging is more than a privilege.

Belonging, I am now convinced, can be a choice.

Sven Werner – Belgium/Luxembourg/Germany

'The German poet Hermann Hesse said something about a magic dwelling in each beginning. I love beginnings,' Sven Werner, the Glasgow-based artist, filmmaker, composer and Scottish BAFTA winner, states with a smile.

He remembers arriving in Scotland for the first time 20 years ago, to work on a project for his Master's thesis. He met his wife then. But his real beginning with Scotland was a decade ago when the couple decided to return to Scotland. 'I was in between projects,' he recalls. 'I borrowed a friend's bicycle and pedalled around the city when I saw this derelict building. There was a fishmonger's shop at street level, but the floor above caught my eye. I approached the owners who were brothers and asked if they'd let me have the place for an art studio.' Intuition prompted him to add, 'And if you can give me a job, too, I'll be able to pay the rent!' His gamble paid off: Sven was offered work both in the fish shop and in the family café across the road. 'I found this amazing chair in the street. Sometimes I used to go upstairs and the space was empty, apart from that one old leather chair. I'd sit and think about the possibilities, still dressed in my fishmonger's overalls. It was a magic beginning, a dream come true.'

Sven Werner cuts a very different figure now. Impeccably dressed in a pressed white shirt, fitted waistcoat and black bow tie, he looks every inch the influential force in the Glasgow underground arts scene that he is. But his enthusiasm for his work is undiminished. 'I have felt nothing but welcomed and supported here,' he states simply. The process was gradual: he created installations and invited people to his studio. The right people saw the work and he began to collaborate with Glasgow's Cryptic, a producing art house focused on developing and presenting the next generation of Scottish and international artists. That in turn led to other exhibitions and opportunities. He succeeded in applying for funding and was able to set up as a full-time artist. Soon his name appeared on shortlists for prestigious cultural events like the Edinburgh Art Festival's Made in Scotland showcase and the British Council showcase.

'Perhaps I inherited my curiosity from my parents who moved around a lot during my childhood,' he muses. 'The concept of the EU just made sense to me. When that concept, which had been so helpful to me, was rejected by the British people, I thought: "What am I doing in a country which doesn't value all of this?" But then I got a letter from my local MSP. I think most EU citizens in Scotland got one. It said, "We want you to stay, we value you." It was a small thing, but it really meant a lot at the time. I still have the letter. It made a huge difference to me.'

Sven is clearly inspired by the landscape and the light he finds here. 'My filmic installation performances have a sort of dark fairy-tale element. Scotland is a great fit for the atmosphere in my work, like two pieces of a jigsaw just slotting together. It was here that I emerged as an artist – first there was curiosity about my work and then full-on support. Now I have an arts and film career. I have a lot to thank Scotland for.'

Arrival

*Give me... a little music played out of doors by somebody
I do not know.* – John Keats

'YOU'LL RECOGNISE HIM. He's really tall,' Louie said.

I raised my eyebrows.

'He'll be there, don't worry.'

I was still unconvinced. 'How will I recognise him if I've never ever met him? Do you have a photo?'

My friend Louie shook his head and giggled, as if suddenly struck by a thought of pure genius. 'Look. He's called Fergus MacNeill, right? And when we worked together in London, he used to really like this song, *Celebration* by Kool & the Gang. That can be your signal.'

'What?'

To me, an uninitiated German about to move to Scotland for the duration of my degree, Louie was the nearest thing to a native: a Londoner, albeit jobbing in Germany, but with a host of useful connections. One of these, his friend Fergus, was to pick me up from Glasgow Airport, drop me at his parents' house overnight and see me onto some sort of transport to Edinburgh the morning after.

Simple and straightforward. But this was Louie.

'Sing the song. That way he'll definitely know it's you.' Louie winked.

I decided to leave it – after all, I didn't want him to think the wind-up was working.

Barely a week later, I'd done the necessary. Guitar and gargantuan backpack stored in the plane's hold, I sat in my seat on the edge of the atmosphere and cried.

I cried for the parents I'd left behind, for my sister about to give birth, for the enormity of my decision – and for the country disappearing under clouds beneath me, which would no longer be my home as soon as I touched down on Scotland's rain-soaked asphalt.

It was dusk. The businessman beside me pushed his way into the queue; in fact, everyone who had dozed and lazed their way through the flight was suddenly in a rush. Except me. Like the landing jolt, it struck me – I wasn't just scared of going. I was scared of arriving! What had possessed me to want to come here?

Guitar and backpack reclaimed, I shuffled through the exit gate. For all these complete strangers knew, I was *naturally* puffy-faced and red-nosed, and I had more important things to worry about anyway: finding Fergus. I scanned the crowd, already thinning with greetings and departures. A couple of men were tall, I guessed. I sauntered past them both. Neither of them paid me the slightest bit of attention.

Waiting alone in an arrivals lounge late at night in a strange country, I began to panic – until it struck me. *Stroke of genius, Louie! Very funny! He's primed Fergus not to declare himself until...*

I took a deep breath. So be it! Picking my guitar up, I sauntered past the first tall man who had sat down by now. Humming, with ever increasing volume as I passed.

He looked up, but not with recognition. With something else I'd rather not think about.

I decided to give the other man a try, even though he was now hugging an elderly woman who'd been on the plane behind me. Singing timidly now: 'Celebration...'

I'm ashamed to admit; I even sang the guitar riff which follows.

Both tall men disappeared down the emptying arrivals lounge, but come to think of it, Louie was small. Maybe, to him, almost anyone would be tall. Nothing for it. '*CELEBRATION...*'

By the time I heard loud footsteps echoing, I was pretty much singing out all my desperation at top volume. A ridiculously tall young man ran into the hall, where by now only a few people milled around – most of them cleaners – and a singing German student. He'd gone to the wrong gate by mistake.

Almost 25 years later, this country has become *my* country. I have arrived. And if you recall a very odd time at Glasgow Airport where a dishevelled teenager spontaneously burst into song, maybe now you understand.

WG Saraband – Portugal

WG Saraband is an interesting man. The Algarve-born artist and political activist based in Edinburgh holds a Master's degree in Medieval History of the Islamic Mediterranean and wrote his thesis on the subject of homosexuality in the literature and poetry of Medieval al-Andalus and the Maghreb.

He knew for a long time that he wanted to leave Portugal. 'There wasn't much of a future there that I could see for my husband (then-boyfriend) and I. We were originally set on going to the Netherlands, and we got on with learning Dutch. I worked as a waiter then, and in the restaurant I used to get loads of Scottish customers, who were incredibly nice for the most part. They kept on saying, "You should come to Scotland, we need people like you." Well, it just so happened that we changed our minds and ended up here instead, so you can blame it on a series of coincidences which changed our lives.' The moment he stepped out of the plane in Edinburgh and inhaled that cold, crisp air, he felt like he had truly come home.

He has certainly made his mark here, both through his art and through his activism for both Scottish independence and LGBT rights. 'Let me put it this way, if I keep going to bed knowing that I'm trying to do my best for Scotland, whatever small part that may be, I'm happy. There have been so many moving memories: being invited to a political event where I got to meet the First Minister, and most recently getting married to the man of my dreams in the Edinburgh City Chambers while we were both wearing full kilts. That was very special.'

It hasn't all been plain sailing. He remembers working for a tech company in Edinburgh where his boss introduced him to sectarianism. 'I got to see how misogynistic and archaic the male-dominated world of tech still is. Shortly after quitting that awful job I launched myself as a full-time artist.'

He also recalls the time around the Brexit referendum: 'It's just that disgusting feeling of being talked about as an immigrant, like some sort of insect that had just invaded the house and needed to be exterminated. I really expected Leave to win, but on the morning of the result I still felt like I had been punched in the stomach at someone's funeral. It was grief, literally.'

His Portuguese heritage is not something he is always conscious of, but he knows it's there. 'There are things that will never change – I may cook haggis, neeps and tatties now, but the whisky sauce that I'm going to make alongside it? There's no way I'm not using Portuguese olive oil as the basis for that. I would panic without any olive oil in my kitchen, I'm not joking, it's the basis for almost every food I cook. As much as I increasingly feel Scottish, my roots are Portuguese, and they always will be. The two identities are not mutually exclusive, fortunately.' He views his new homeland with striking confidence and has a message for Scotland.

'See those imperfections you have? Every other nation does too. It doesn't mean you aren't allowed to love yourself and to see yourself with the same dignity as everyone else.'

2

Blackpool

To unpathed waters, undreamed shores. – Shakespeare

MY STORY WITH Scotland actually began two years before the incident at Glasgow Airport. I was working in a café in Blackpool. Yes, you read right. When I was nine years old, my older sister presented her new boyfriend to the family. An Englishman seemed so very, very exotic in small-town Germany, with his permed hair and his Mini Cooper. To cut a long story short, they married and settled in Germany and Allan, hailing from Blackpool, offered to help when I approached the usual rite of passage for all late-teen Germans worth their salt: spend time abroad to improve your English. 'Head to Blackpool,' he suggested. 'There's plenty of work going there over the summer!'

He was right, of course. After a few expensive phone calls, I hopped on a Eurolines coach to London, crouched against a concrete wall in Victoria Coach Station for a few hours and caught a National Express bus north. Allan's friends became my friends and I stayed with Will and Anne for a couple of summers. I was astounded at the British way of securing a summer job. In Germany it was all about numbers and certificates and references. Here I simply dressed up in a tidy and ironed outfit, put on some heels, brushed my hair, applied lipstick and hit the pavement. I walked from café to restaurant to hotel along the Promenade. By evening, I had several offers of employment and elected, for my sins, to join an establishment called The Bispham Kitchen, a fish and chips restaurant a short bike ride from my hosts' home.

As I waited on tables and wiped greasy trays, my mind was somewhere else altogether. *What was I going to do with my life?* I was a year away from my final exams, the Abitur. One thing was certain: I wanted to go to university. I pondered my options. There were a few courses and places which appealed to me back in Germany, but wanderlust was my defining characteristic then and I had begun to dream of Scotland. Could I possibly contemplate a degree there?

The seed of the idea was planted, and I could not help it – it grew new shoots every day. But weren't tuition fees extortionate? What would my parents say if their youngest fled the nest and crossed several borders in the process? Was I being unreasonable by wanting an education as well as an adventure? Was I selfish?

My faith is generally the lens through which I contemplate life, so praying seemed the natural response to all of these concerns. I don't remember the exact words, but my prayer went something like, 'God, if coming abroad is the right thing to do, I have no idea how to go about it. Please show me.' It may not have been articulate, but it was earnestly prayed. I felt more peaceful.

The next day I was clearing tables in the restaurant. The midday rush had passed, and a single customer remained sitting at a table with a pile of paperwork. In the background, the soundtrack to *Doctor Zhivago* warbled through the air for the millionth time – I had long ceased to hear it.

'Busy day?' she asked.

I dropped a rattling handful of knives and forks onto my tray. 'Not too bad, thanks.'

'Where are you from?' she asked, lifting her head.

'Germany. I'm just working here for the summer.' I smiled. This was a little more interest than I usually got from the customers.

'Are you still at school?'

I nodded, carrying my plates past her towards the kitchen. 'Only another year.'

When I returned, she had dropped her pen and closed her books. 'What are you going to do after school?'

I was starting to feel a little exposed, as if someone was taking a magnifying glass to my dreams. But her eyes were kind. 'I was hoping to study literature, actually. And probably English.'

She narrowed her eyes. A shiver ran up my spine as my prayer from the day before shot through my mind.

She spoke thoughtfully and with genuine warmth. 'Are you going to study in Germany? Or have you considered coming over here?'

Truthfully, time had stopped for me for a moment. 'As a matter of fact, it did cross my mind,' I shrugged, feigning nonchalance.

'Well, I'm a careers advisor and my job is to advise our sixth formers on which universities to apply to. Would you like to pop by my office and take a few prospectuses?'

I was speechless, but she simply handed me a card. I recognised the imposing Fylde College building on the logo. The very next day I cycled over. I recall very little of the actual conversation, but I do recall the wobbly ride home, plastic bags tearing with the weight of paper dangling from both handlebars.

My host family got on board enthusiastically. 'There is a man who lives at the end of the street – he has a reputation for knowing everything there is to know about universities in the UK. He'll be a great one to talk to.'

I don't remember the gentleman's name. But I do remember that he elaborated for half the evening on his fondness for the Alastair Cooke radio programme *Letter From America* which he even took the trouble of recording for me later. For the rest of the time he pored over prospectuses. 'Hmm, English. Language or Literature? Both, I'd recommend.'

I nodded.

'BA or MA – MA is preferable, without a doubt.'

I nodded again.

'Campus or city?'

I looked at him uncertainly. I had never heard the word 'campus' before.

'I mean, would you prefer a university where you are based on a self-sufficient campus area, or one where you'll be based in the middle of a city or town?'

My voice became stronger. 'City or town. Yes, definitely.'

'And then there is the question of your grades.'

I breathed a little easier. My projected results were pretty good. In Germany, I could have had my pick. I was on course for A grades, I told him. But I balked when the gentleman began pushing for Oxford or Cambridge – this was not what I had in mind.

'I was thinking perhaps Scotland...' I began.

Far from judging my impulsive leanings, he simply caught the ball I had thrown him and ran with it. 'Scotland, yes, yes.'

He began to list the Scottish universities on a piece of paper, a memento I would hold on to for decades afterwards. 'I'll mark out the ones which will be hard to get into.' His heavy biro scratched the capital letter H for 'hard' beside Edinburgh, St Andrews and Glasgow. I gulped.

'But my grades...'

'It's not just your grades, my dear. It's your statement! A teacher will have to write something about you. A sort of reference, about two pages long.'

'What?' I had never heard anything so ridiculous. My English teacher back in Germany was a competent man, but I wasn't sure at all whether he would be enthusiastic about this! And I thoroughly disliked the idea of my fate resting in my teacher's hands back home. If only the Higher Education enthusiast in front of me could have written it!

By the end of the night, it was done. Glasgow didn't offer the right course, so my applications would go to St Andrews, Edinburgh and Aberdeen, with two north of England universities as backup – after all I had friends in the north.

One prayer, three days, two encounters with strangers – and the path ahead seemed clear.

Now all I needed to do was to persuade my parents.

Professor Daniela Sime – Romania

'Daniela! There's a lady on the phone. She is speaking English,' Daniela Sime's brother shouted.

The caller was a teacher from the University of St Andrews. 'Quick, find the atlas,' the young Daniela motioned to her sibling. 'Find out where St Andrews is!' The likeable academic laughs as she recalls: 'I had been offered a scholarship to study abroad, but I had to secure an offer from a university within days. One of my friends had said: "Hey, if you need to find out about universities abroad, you can use this thing called the internet…" The St Andrews teacher called soon after and just like that, in 1998, I came to Scotland.'

Sime got her PhD in Education at the University of Stirling and is now Professor of Youth, Migration and Social Justice at the University of Strathclyde, with research interests in social justice and inequalities, migration, young people's education and equal opportunities. Talking about her contribution to Scotland, Daniela explains, 'I would hope that I am influencing students to reflect on the type of society they want to live in, in terms of inclusivity and inequality; to ask themselves: "What can *I* do to make things better?" I am also involved in a range of initiatives as a volunteer, like mentoring young people. I was very fortunate to benefit from incredible generosity from the people I met since I first came to Scotland. I can't ever pay it back, but I can pay it forward! In my own practice, I try to replicate that caring attitude towards my students and the people in the communities I work in.'

Daniela wears her Romanian heritage lightly: home is now in Scotland. 'I feel very settled here. It's usually other people who remind you that you still sound different – like when they ask where I'm from, although I know it's usually just a well-meaning question.' She has a daughter born here, who describes herself as half Scottish, a quarter Romanian and a quarter Catalan due to Sime's husband.

In her view, the referendum and the UK's narrow decision to leave the EU was a sad occasion and led to a rise in aggression and xenophobia for many. Some of the children she interviewed for research were told by their parents not to speak their home language in public, to try and 'blend in' more.

On one occasion Sime was meeting a friend in town. 'We were surrounded by five or six kids. They can't have been older than eight or nine, but they threw popcorn at us and shouted, "Fuck off back to your country!" Incidents like these reinforce to me that we can't be complacent; we still have work to do. People learn to hate and xenophobia needs addressing. Encouragingly, we seem to be making progress in Scotland – according to the latest PISA (Programme for International Student Assessment) study, in Scotland, children's understanding of global issues has improved significantly, and they are more inclusive in their views than children in many other countries.'

The academic is hopeful in relation to Scotland's future: 'Scotland is making an effort to be pro-EU and pro-immigration – and it goes beyond the economic argument that we need workers from abroad. It's about identity and the kind of country we want to be. I'm glad I picked Scotland.' She pauses for thought briefly. 'Actually, she picked me.'

3

Parents

*As long as you have the blessing of your parents it does not matter
even if you live in the mountains.* – Greek proverb

BEING THE YOUNGEST had its advantages. Over the decades, Papa and Mama had done their fighting with my older sisters. Consequently, my parents' approach to anything they didn't approve of was benign neglect. For example, when I started going out with a young man my parents disapproved of, any mention of him was met by serene silence and a swift change of topic. Through simple non-engagement, they presumably thought, all of this would go away – it was a well-tested method.

From time to time they tried a more head-on approach: 'There are plenty of good universities here, Barbara,' my father intoned as he left the room. 'And we are not going to give you more money than we did your sisters…'

'Understood. Well, I've applied to Edinburgh, St Andrews, Aberdeen…'

'Yes, yes.'

My parents' faith in my haplessness was touching. They assumed I would take the whole moving abroad idea no further without their management, but I was properly invested by now, relentlessly pursuing my teachers, my school and various education authorities to provide the necessary paperwork.

'You'll have to pay fees,' my mother countered.

I waved a typed A5 insert from the handbook published by the German Academic Exchange Service. 'Look, Mum: It says here that whole-degree student fees will be covered by the EU from this academic year. Lucky, eh?' It was such a new announcement that it had not even made it into the printed version of the handbook. My parents remained sceptical.

No precedent? That sounded like a risky manoeuvre. Reckless in fact. But with the unmatched arrogance of youth, I pressed on undeterred.

My English teacher asked me, of all people, to proofread his reference for me: 'Your English is almost as good as mine. Just look over it, okay?' I in turn sought his help with my personal statement. One thing hasn't changed since then: however long I tinker with words, there is always the worry that I have missed something. But with a looming deadline, I sent off my UCAS application and waited, taking a fact-finding trip to the University of Heidelberg in order to assure my parents that there was a plan B. The truth is that by then, the damage was done. I had read and absorbed too much about Scotland and its history. I was hooked.

Many evenings in my room were spent looking at old photographs of a trip I barely remembered: a decade before, visiting Edinburgh with my parents, sister and soon-to-be-brother-in-law. We had stayed in university accommodation just off the iconic Royal Mile. Rain-glaze reflected off the cobblestones beneath stirred up skies. The photographs were mostly dark and grainy. But if I was to spend the next four years of my life away from here, why not in a country which appealed to me in that moody, romantic way? Besides, if I was to study English in Germany, it would remain a foreign language course. The thought of studying the subject with a literature focus, in an interesting new culture appealed so much more.

In February, the first reply sailed through the door. I remember it distinctly – a brown A4 envelope with a foreign stamp, promisingly substantial. 'The University of Aberdeen' proclaimed a stamp beneath. *Probably too heavy to be a rejection*, I speculated hopefully as I weighed it carefully in my hand and made my way to the dining table. My mother, so far a shining example of the 'don't engage' school of parenting, watched from the kitchen door. A rip and a shake and I could barely believe it: I was in! 'Is that all they want?' I mumbled as I read the details of the offer. It was a conditional, but under the German system at the time, less depended on my final exams. I had all but met the conditions already. I had been offered a place. I was going to Scotland!

With a sigh, my stoical mother came to give me a hug of resigned blessing and I hugged her back hard. It was happening. It was really happening.

St Andrews declined the pleasure of my company for four years. I am ashamed to say it stung – not because I had my heart set on St Andrews above all others, but because I was not used to failing. Before I even got there, Scotland was teaching me lessons in life. However, not long after, the envelope I had been waiting for followed. The University of Edinburgh.

The memories are still vivid: the sound of the tear, the smooth slide of the paper, the blur as my eyes adjusted to the words, the split-second of incredulity at the requirements. These conditions were even less taxing than Aberdeen's – and definitely achievable! Most of all, I remember the cheer that ripped from my lungs and through the house.

I did not hesitate, nor did I wait for offers from any other institutions. Edinburgh it was, and I sent my acceptance letter back almost immediately (inconveniently, these were the days before emails). I would study English Language and English Literature, and the degree was an MA, with joint honours – provided I could cope with the work.

Looking back, there was a dreamlike quality about that spring. My final exams, learning to drive, working in a care home over the summer to save up funds for university, swift arrangements for travel and transfers, farewells and festivities. Change was afoot.

Martin Cingel – Slovakia

'When I first arrived in Edinburgh as an ice hockey player, I was sure I would be here for eight months or so. It was a stepping-stone. But that's not how it turned out! Nearly 20 years later and I am still here,' he laughs. The Slovakian's cheerfulness is infectious.

He is extremely fond of his adopted homeland. 'The thing is, wherever you go in the world – and I have travelled a lot – when you mention Scotland, everyone goes "Wow!" It is one of the most beautiful countries in the world and the Scots welcome you with open arms. If you want to make friends around the globe, just say you're from Scotland!'

He vividly remembers those early days of playing for Edinburgh Capitals Ice Hockey Club. His wife had just arrived in Scotland for his first match. 'I was in the changing room with the guys, but she knew no one. No one at all. But when she made her way into the families' lounge at Murrayfield, several people got up to welcome her and to ask her to sit with them. I have never forgotten that, and I will always be grateful. Those people are still family friends today.'

His children are fluent Slovakian speakers. When asked in school whether he was a Scot, his son answered that he was a 'proud Slovakian born in Scotland'. In the run-up to the 2014 independence referendum, he remembers the dads on the touchline while watching his kids play football. 'They said: "Hey, Martin, you come from a country who split. How was it when Slovakia broke away from the larger Czech Republic?" I told them that it took 15 years or so for the country to find its feet, but that it was fine after that. We were the same, a small country breaking away from a bigger one, and around the same population.'

The EU referendum two years later was different. Martin felt that leaving the EU would be a bad move for Scotland. 'My nine-year-old kids were coming home from school talking about Brexit, and worried about what would happen. Nine years old! We had to explain to them that, although we were disappointed on a personal level, this was a democracy. If people vote for something in a democracy, it will happen. It's the price you pay for free speech without fear of the consequences. But our opportunity to come to Scotland existed because of the EU, and we as a family have benefited. It'll be much more difficult for others now.'

UK sports fans, too, have benefited from Martin's presence here. He has given much joy to viewers as an elite sportsman and now brings his experience and expertise to the coaching team for the UK Under 18s ice hockey players with whom he won gold in their World Championship division in 2018. 'Definitely one of the best moments in my career!' he finishes emphatically.

4

Uncertainty

There is no shame in not knowing; the shame lies in not finding out. –
Russian proverb

AFTER A NIGHT in Glasgow, another friend-of-a-friend picked me up to drive me to Edinburgh. I remember the gentleman's name as Paul, who drove me straight to the house of Norah Nicoll, a widow who had a house on Clermiston Hill. This was my way of acclimatising; Freshers' Week would not begin until the week after. I had six days to cajole my brain into speaking English, to get used to Scottish accents – and to sort out my funding. By a very happy coincidence, the offices of the Student Awards Agency for Scotland were located in the same part of town, a simple bus ride away. Norah also had a lodger, a young Irish student called Helen whom I liked. Of course, I was the newcomer while Helen had her ready-made social life in full swing.

It so happened that homesickness landed a blow from behind. I hadn't expected it so soon (if in my conceit I had expected it at all), but here I was, battling tearfulness in a stranger's living room. The television was on, tuned to some sort of church service. I think it must have been *Songs of Praise*.

Back in Germany, my sister had given birth days after I left – a baby girl I wouldn't now see until at least Christmas time. I felt exhausted by the constant concentration of speaking a foreign language, frustrated by missing the subtleties of humour and bereft of friends. All these people around me were helpful and polite and kind, but it was clear to me that I would be no permanent fixture in their lives, nor they in mine. I would move on, like a dried-up autumn leaf which blows into an open kitchen door and is swept right out again. I didn't *really* know anybody in Scotland. I didn't even know many people in the UK as a whole: my brother-in-law Allan didn't count as he was living in Germany. His brother Dave, my Blackpool host family, and there it ended, pretty much. What was I doing here?

It was at that point that something caught my attention. A word, a turn of phrase, or perhaps just the voice, but I looked up and there, spread huge across the TV screen – I couldn't believe it – was Dave. Yes, Allan's brother. I had been aware that he was a Church of England vicar, but I had never seen him in all his regalia before. Preaching peace from a pulpit in the very living room I was staying in, at the very minute the television was tuned to that very channel, at the very moment when I needed it most. Some people say there are no coincidences – and I was beginning to believe it. I found out later that that it was the first and last time he was ever on television.

The episode reminded me of the lady in the Blackpool café, and I breathed a little easier. I would be okay. People are people the world over. With a little time and patience, I would make friends.

With hindsight, it's strange what sticks in the mind. I remember that Sunday lunch. I had never had cheese soufflé before – I had never even heard of it! Mrs Nicoll served it up with pride and suggested we'd go for a walk afterwards. *Yes*, I thought, *something to do*. Acclimatising and adjusting to a new culture is so much harder when you are sat on your bed thinking of home. I grabbed my jacket and off we went.

The stroll took us onto a wooded hill not too far away. The path curved and snaked through the trees and in the distance, I could hear the Edinburgh traffic thunder in the valley. *How many other students were spending the last weekend of the holidays with their families before making the journey to the Scottish capital?* Even thinking of it as a capital was odd – the wooded path felt so remote, so otherworldly, with the autumn sun weaving through swaying branches, leaves colouring with golden tinges. Little did I know that things were about to get a whole lot stranger. The wood thinned a little to reveal a fence and a field of grass, slightly sloped. I stopped, suddenly. Mrs Nicoll and her lodger walked on, but I stayed rooted to the spot, a frown furrowing my forehead.

No, my eyes did not deceive me. There was a whole group of zebras on that hill.

I ignored the giggles from further up the path and tried to see more clearly, shading my eyes. The zebras were still there, but in the field beside them there was also something like...

'Ah, very funny,' I finally scolded, realising Helen and my landlady were by now doubled over with laughter. 'It's a zoo, right? Zebras and wildebeest are not your typical Scottish wildlife; even I know that!' I marched up to them. Mrs Nicoll's eyes shone with glee.

'She does that to everyone,' Helen chuckled. 'It threw me too.'

The following day I set out for the offices of the Student Awards Agency Scotland, the body dealing with fees and student finance.

I won't lie; I felt considerable trepidation as I approached the doors of the nondescript office building. I had no appointment, but this is where I had been advised to go in order guarantee that my tuition fees were indeed going to be covered, in their entirety, by the European Union. The academic year of 1991–92 was going to be the inaugural year of that particular arrangement, and all I had to testify to this was the by now crumpled paper insert into the brochure of the German Academic Exchange Service.

Now, this could go two ways. Either I would be waved through an open door, commence my studies as planned and return to Germany four years later with an MA in English Language and Literature. Or, alternatively, I would pack my bags again that very week, lose my deposit with Pollock Halls of Residence, spend the last of my cash on a flight home and crawl to the nearest university that would have me back in Germany. There was no middle ground.

I stated my name and handed over the paperwork from the University of Edinburgh. The woman behind the desk mumbled something I didn't understand. She waved over a colleague and then another. By that time, I was shuffling from foot to foot and beads of sweat were forming on my forehead. I barely heard her when she called my name. 'Miss Haas? That's it all in order now.'

I struggled to comprehend. Stay or go, money or no money, study or not study? I wished these people would keep it simple for the foreigner. But there was a smile, enough to render a thousand words unnecessary. 'The European Union pays your fees,' she clarified in patronisingly slow words. I think I remember her stamping my document with a flourish, or I may be making that bit up. One thing, however, was finally certain.

I was going to study here in Edinburgh. A strange calm settled on me on the way back to my lodgings. On the way, I squinted to see if I could spot the zebras on the hill from my bus window, but no such luck.

Krystyna Irena Szumelukowa – Poland

'I have always been aware of my Polish heritage, but I do not think of myself as a "foreigner" which tends to presume a negative and potentially hostile connotation,' says Krystyna Irena Szumelukowa who was born stateless in the aftermath of the Second World War. Her parents, both Polish-born but then displaced, came to the UK under the Polish Resettlement Act of 1947. Despite achieving a First Class Honours degree in Geography from King's College London, the young Krystyna was debarred from her entitlement to sit the entrance examination to the Civil Service, because her parents were 'born behind the Iron Curtain', so she pursued a career in local government instead. She arrived in Scotland in 1994 to take up the position of Director of Economic Development and Estates with the Edinburgh District Council where she became instrumental in setting up the new partnership with the city of Kraków.

Throughout her quarter-century in Scotland's capital, Krystyna has contributed to Scottish society in a range of ways: through her town planning and economic development career in local government; in private practice as a management consultant including work as Planning Reporter with the Scottish Government; as an international election observer for the OSCE (Organisation for Security and Co-operation in Europe); and as a trustee of Edinburgh World Heritage. She is currently associated with the General Council of the University of Edinburgh and has invested much of her energy in UK– Scotland–Poland relationships. In addition, she became vice-chair of the Scottish–Polish Cultural Association in Edinburgh and established Zielony Balonik (2006), a book club that specialises in the reading of contemporary Polish literature.

Perhaps most memorably, she was a founding trustee of the Wojtek Memorial Trust which sought to honour the unique heroism of Wojtek the 'Polish Soldier Bear' and of Polish soldiers in the Second World War. Planning consent was granted for a memorial in Princes Street Gardens in Edinburgh, with Krystyna principally responsible for the management of the planning process and funding for the project. 'At times it was a struggle to deliver, but no pain, no gain as the saying goes,' she recalls cheerfully. The opening of the monument, 7 November 2015, is still a very moving memory: 'I can still see it now: the unveiling of the Wojtek

Memorial in Princes Street Gardens in Edinburgh in torrential rain and the Polish flag flying above Edinburgh Castle by permission of the First Minister.'

She remembers the feelgood atmosphere in Edinburgh on the day when the new Scottish Parliament was opened by the Queen, but also the despair she felt when she awoke to hear the news of the outcome of the Brexit referendum.

'It felt as if my whole career had been rejected because I am a European. Throughout my career, I had endeavoured to make whatever contribution I could to foster a cohesive and peaceful Europe and to achieve a greater understanding of different cultures. The rhetoric and lies of the Brexit campaigners horrified me, and still do to this day. I would encourage Scotland to take pride in the words of Robert Burns: "The man's the gowd for a' that"; to continue to strive for the delivery of modern, local, democratic and egalitarian values.'

5

University

There are no foreign lands. It is the traveller only who is foreign. –
Robert Louis Stevenson

MY ARRIVAL IN halls was probably atypical – the sprawl of Pollock
Halls at the foot of Arthur's Seat was to be home for the next year,
but my vision of a corridor full of ready-made friendship candidates
didn't quite materialise. I had been dropped off by gentleman Paul who
was kind enough to take time out of his busy day to drive me in from
Corstorphine. It didn't take long to wrestle my blue backpack out of
the boot and slide my guitar out through the back door. I thanked him
for everything. 'Guess this is it. Good luck,' he smiled.

Instead of following the steady stream of students to the front door, I
was directed to a flat at the bottom of Lee House. It had been a former
warden's residence. 'There'll be another couple of students living in there
with you,' I was told. 'Just go on in.'

There was a more than a whiff of disappointment in my steps as I
entered the empty flat. I could hear shrieking and laughing from the
open windows above me as newly arrived students greeted their also
newly arrived corridor neighbours. I pictured them, mingling naturally
as they carried boxes from their parents' cars and held doors open for
each other. Their fathers and mothers would nod to each other politely.
They might even make small talk in the lifts. *Traffic's hellish out there.*
Nice day though.

Twenty minutes later I sat on my own on the edge of my strange bed
in my empty flat, away from the hubbub of the floors above. Unpacking
had taken six minutes. I waited.

I don't know how long I sat there like that, until there was a scratching at the flat door – yes, it was unmistakeable: someone was trying to turn a key. There were voices, too. I rushed to open the door.

Annabelle was Canadian and gracefully tall, with a confidence I envied from the moment we met. Pharmacology. Her father was an academic and travelled all the time. She was famished. 'My parents are staying at the Sheraton, so we are going there for dinner,' she announced, her blonde hair whipping past me as she left. 'See you later!'

The next day our little flat would be complete with Elena, the daughter of an Italian government official. Her boyfriend was a professional footballer for Roma and she walked in with several hangers of ballgowns ahead of her suitcases. Both of them were cheery and fun-loving, and I liked them. Still, as I blu-tacked photographs of my German friends up on the wardrobe (the only place where blu-tack was allowed. Incidentally, blu-tack was utterly new to me too – a source of much amusement to my flatmates. I had never come across the stuff!), I was certain – these girls were unlikely to be my gang.

But who was?

Sometimes there is nothing for it but to be brave. Freshers' Week was for people like me after all. I joined a pub crawl (another new concept – binge drinking seemed strange to someone who had been legally allowed to drink since the age of 16). One of my new 'friends' ended up sleeping on my floor one night – she simply couldn't remember where she lived. At the Freshers' Fair where students could join societies they were interested in, I signed on the dotted line for Amnesty International, the Christian Union and a volleyball team – and my very first ceilidh, held in none other than the imposing and beautiful McEwen Hall, normally reserved for graduations.

I approached on my own. The door was open and cheery faces waved us in, with traditional Scottish music playing through the speakers. I don't remember what I wore or which day of the week it was, but I do remember a Glaswegian announcer called 'Wee Pete'. That was the moment I realised that some people – ie the ones from Glasgow – spoke a kind of English that bore absolutely no resemblance to the language I considered myself fairly fluent in. Oh true, he opened his mouth and sounds came out. Others nodded and laughed at various points during the short speeches, but to me he may as well have been speaking Mandarin. I looked around. If anyone else felt like me, they were doing a good job of hiding it. Still, you wear your smile most boldly when it matters most. Every last one of the people gathered here was a potentially like-minded friend, a companion-in-waiting. I tried to observe the dance steps. Wee Pete's instructions washed over me like white noise, but I could surely copy what everybody else was doing, couldn't I? I was fairly musical. This was music, wasn't it? I think I danced every dance, struck up conversations with complete strangers, laughed, smiled, let my hair fly in the spins. Red-faced and out of breath, I chatted by the water fountain and re-joined the fray. I vaguely remember dancing with some fourth year medic called Derek, somebody called Hugh, somebody called Cliff. I also danced with a skinny second year in a checked flannel shirt. The reason I remember that is that I would marry him three years later.

But on that night, none of that entered my head. As the last chords rang out and Wee Pete said something that presumably meant goodbye, there was a communal awkward moment. All the older students found their friends and filed out together while the rest of us stood like single rabbits in the glaring light which had just been switched on. I hadn't even thought about it, but now that I *was* thinking about it, I wasn't at all sure that I would find my way back to halls. How late was it?

These very same thoughts must have been replicated across the hall. There was a little half-hearted shuffling towards the exit, until a Northern Irish voice hollered out loudly above every other sound. 'Anyone heading back to Pollock?'

Yep!' said someone.

I shouted my relief. 'Yes, me.'

'Me too.'

'And me.'

There must have been around ten of us, weaving back towards halls through Newington, chatting as if we had known each other all our lives. The Northern Irish hollerer turned out to be Chris, from Londonderry. He now lives and works in the US. Sharon, another fellow marcher in the makeshift group, later became my bridesmaid and lifelong pal. If I remember clearly, we actually climbed Arthur's Seat late that night and hugged each other to keep warm in the darkness before the sun rose majestically the next morning, bathing the city in promise.

In the coming days we began to sit together in the refectory, wait for each other as we headed to lectures and popped into each other's rooms with fake errands, just to have a chat. I know they called me 'the German one'. Mostly, I could follow conversations and although I was no match for Chris or his fellow Irishman Dickie in terms of quick wit, I broadly understood the jokes and laughed along. I had to unlearn some of my Germanic literalness and let go, trusting in the vibe rather than the words, and amazingly, it worked.

It took only hours for us to form a firm friendship group and mere days for a few extras to join us, including the skinny flannel shirt wearer they called Rob. I began to look forward to each new day in Edinburgh.

This was going to be fun.

Professor Sir Anton Muscatelli – Italy

Teacher. Researcher. Academic leader. Economist. Contributor to public policy. Anton Muscatelli has certainly worn many hats. The Principal of the University of Glasgow came to Scotland as a teenager in the mid-'70s and has made his mark on the country he calls home. 'I'm not a politician and I've advised governments of all political colours in Scotland and the UK. I'm proud that I've tried to do that without taking sides in political debates. The only time I did was around the Brexit referendum and its aftermath, largely because of the overwhelming views in my university community, the impact of Brexit on its vital interests and the negative effects of Brexit on the economy. I've tried my best to give the best advice on economic policy to whichever government or public body has sought it – I do believe in the importance of academics providing public service.'

Muscatelli saw that the Leave campaign had real traction while visiting a number of northern English cities like Liverpool and Newcastle. 'I realised that the pro-Leave sentiments were extremely strong. And then of course on the night of the vote, when the first results started coming in from the north-east of England, I realised my fears were coming true.'

His loyalty is to Scotland, but he describes his Italian heritage as very important: 'And as time passes, it becomes more important still. You become more aware of your roots, and more attracted to them. The issue of identity is very complex. I do feel as if I have more than one identity now. At the same time, like many first-generation immigrants, you end up feeling as if you don't completely belong either in your country of origin or in your adopted country.'

There came a point when the young man's identity became a matter of choice. 'My parents and the rest of my family decided to leave Scotland and the UK to return to Italy. I was 20 years old at the time and had begun university. That was a moment when I had to decide for myself what my future was going to be – and having decided to stay here, I felt a cord had been cut.' As a foreign national in the early 1980s when he graduated, Muscatelli was barred from choosing certain careers which he considered applying for: the Civil Service and the Central Bank were not open to European Economic Community graduates.

Muscatelli's history with Scotland is full of anecdotes, mostly about his struggle to understand the Scottish accent or the context of common expressions. 'I remember trying to catch a train at 3.45pm and asking the attendant when the next train to Glasgow city centre was due. He said, "Ten to", meaning, of course, ten minutes to the hour, so in about five minutes time. I had never heard this expression and instead understood it as "ten two", as in 10.02(pm). I shouted incredulously: "Ten two!" and walked away despondent. He must have thought I was very strange...'

Several decades later, the Principal reflects: 'Scotland has simply been a welcoming country to me. It has given me a world-class education and made me feel at home. There is a huge amount that Scotland can and does offer the world.'

6

Life Lessons

It is the mark of an educated mind to be able to entertain a thought without accepting it. – Aristotle

I WAS ACADEMIC enough, but any studious ambition was very much second to having a good time. English Language held my interest, and basic sentence analysis came easily to me. After all, I had learned English as a foreign language, so an analytical approach was already ingrained. I was astonished that many of my British fellow students struggled with basic parts of speech and had trouble identifying subordinate clauses. To my surprise, the lead lecturer for syntax in the English Language department was an academic called Heinz Giegerich. Judging by his name and accent, he was a fellow German, and here he was, lecturing native speakers in the mechanics of their own language! I was awestruck.

But the course I was most excited about was literature – Scottish Literature to be exact. On a whim, I had decided to choose it over the more mainstream English Literature. If I was going to be part of this country, even if only for four years, I felt I should take the opportunity to immerse myself in its back catalogue a little. How hard could it be?

Fairly challenging, it turned out – Henryson's *The Testament of Cresseid* is about a million miles away from anything you may hear in a German secondary school classroom. In tutorials, I felt like I was surrounded by roomfuls of Glaswegian Wee Petes, discussing things I wasn't party to, in guttural tones that no German schoolteacher would be capable of producing.

One of my very first tutorials focused on Robert Burns – who had ever heard of him? – and his poem *The Cotter's Saturday Night*. I will never forget it. We had each been assigned to lead the discussion on a poem – this particular day, it was the turn of an American student called Maddie whom I could just about understand. The tutor was a cheerful, crop-cut academic called Aileen who was commonly seen cycling around the university in colourful baggy trousers. In any text we studied, even in Burns' poetry, she'd invariably find the feminist angle.

'Well, I thought since this is Scottish literature and a Scottish poet, I should bring some oatcakes and cheese for us all,' Maddie drawled. Her accent stood in sharp contrast to the words she was reading, but what I remember is the rapture with which her oatcakes were received by our tutor. I was not the only one who felt this – there was a little eye rolling and some raised eyebrows as the American and the academic were having an oatcake-induced mutual appreciation session over the poetry of the bard. I had never eaten an oatcake, or heard of Robert Burns, nor did I have the faintest idea what a cotter was – but I loved the descriptions of the devout simplicity of the household in the poem. I related, longed for the peace and tranquillity it so sentimentally describes. It was a world I had never encountered, but I wanted to think about it, dwell on it, learn about it.

The reading list for my course was extensive, but I discovered that it didn't need to be expensive. A tip-off sent me to the second-hand book shops of Edinburgh's West Port. There was also one I really liked by the Old Dick vet school. I would appear with my reading list, and instead of browsing, I simply played helpless to the bookseller: 'Do you have any of these?'

It didn't take long before I was laden with old-fashioned volumes bearing the marks of decades of ownership. I didn't mind one bit. It was a badge of honour to walk into a lecture with a beautiful, bound and foil-lettered copy when all other students held the same soulless Penguin Classics edition. Theirs had academic notes and consistent page numbering and helpful diagrams – but mine had soul. Mine had lived a life, and I was their next custodian.

My favourite lecturer by a mile was a mild-mannered, softly spoken man called Professor Ian Campbell. His specialism was Victorian literature. At the time I was no use at detecting accents, but I wonder now where he hailed from – there was a song in his voice as he delivered his well-worded analysis and wisdom. I looked forward to his lectures. One of the very first I remember was on Kailyard literature – sentimental portrayals of rural

Scotland – and on George Douglas Brown's subversion of that genre in *The House with the Green Shutters*. I was about halfway into the text and felt excited and relatively well prepared for the lecture. Frustratingly, I was also late. The shame of the very front row beckoned, the seats only frequented by those who have no other choice, or by those so hopelessly uncool that they know no better. I slid down into my seat as Professor Campbell began to speak.

Reaching into my bag for a notepad and pen, I also retrieved my highlighted and annotated book, a gloriously aged affair from one of my many charity shop trips.

The talking from the front of the class stopped.

I raised my head. Professor Campbell was staring at me. In fact, every single person in the room was staring at me as a result. 'What is that?' he asked gently.

I looked around me, but no, he had clearly addressed me. 'My book,' I offered weakly.

'May I see it?' he asked. There was an edge in his voice, behind his politeness.

I proffered the book with trembling hand. A quick flick through the opening pages seemed to elicit a hint of a nod, as to himself. 'May I please buy it?' the professor uttered, barely audible.

'Erm, it's quite old... and I've already annotated it...'

Once more he flicked through the pages as I completed my sentence. '... in pen.'

My lecturer grimaced to the room at large as if I had landed a physical blow. There was a pause before he spoke again: 'This young lady has got a first edition of *The House with the Green Shutters*.' There were murmurs. 'And she has marked it in pen! In PEN.' Now there were ripples of laughter. I can't even blame my fellow students – I would have laughed too. I wanted the ground to swallow me up, or for a plane en route to Germany to throw down a hook and conveniently whisk me from this place where I had disgraced myself, so early in the year too. But Professor Campbell was not laughing. He shook his head and repeated, louder: 'Again, I would like to buy this book.' He fumbled in his jacket pocket and produced a crisp banknote. 'I will give you this £20 note for your book, and I will also give you my own new and unmarked paperback copy of *The House with the Green Shutters*. Agreed?'

There was only one speedy way out of this situation. I am not proud of it, but I took it.

'All right. Okay.'

He conducted the swiftest of book exchanges right beneath my nose, as if the banknote from his jacket pocket had been waiting there for this very purpose, and seamlessly picked up the flow of his lecture, a small smile playing about his lips.

I, defeated, sat in the front row – a new celebrity for failing to recognise a first edition when it stared me in the face.

My prize?

I joined the soulless club, shuffling out with my nondescript paperback and a new determination to examine my charity shop finds with more diligence in the future.

* * *

Another memorable encounter with one of my lecturers came a few months later. I had long made peace with Scottish weather – my own part of Germany was prone to persistent rain – but that day was as stormy as they come. Another professor in the literature department, only known by his initials as RDS Jack (his colleagues called him Ronnie), was a regular on the lecture circuit. He was clearly a brilliant mind. I loved his academic writing, with lucid analysis and unexpected but impressive cross-referencing. However, in the flesh, he seemed more than a little eccentric, and sometimes absent-minded. I often struggled to follow his train of thought. He would wander from one end of the DHT (David Hume Tower – now called 40 George Square) lecture room to the other, periodically stopping right in front of an unsuspecting student, and talking down at them without pausing for breath. He was a diminutive man, but I was terrified of him – and I don't think I was the only one.

On that very windy day, I picked my way back from the university area towards the halls of residence when I recognised Professor Jack in front of me, furtively battling his way through the storm, his long coat billowing in the wind. Instinctively, I slowed my steps to avoid awkwardness. He probably wouldn't recognise me, but it wasn't worth the risk.

Out of the corner of my eye, I noticed something high up on the scaffolding which encased a building on St Patrick Square. A contractor's sign was beginning to move – not flutter in the wind, no – it was too solid for that. It was moving in a way it shouldn't. I do not know why the human brain slows moments like this so we experience maximum horror, but the sign swung out in slow motion, flipped around into the air, detached from the scaffold to which it had been fixed and became a toy to the winds. Like a kite out of control, it spun through the air, a piece of board at least half the size of a common door. Mesmerised, I watched as it twirled twice and then hurled itself directly at the head of my professor walking on the pavement below. I shouted, of course, but all sound was lost in the stirring of the storm. I did, however, hear the thud. Right in front of me, my professor was knocked clear off his feet and the next thing I remember is kneeling by his motionless shape on the very pavement I had so often seen frequented by rats at night.

'Sir, are you all right? Professor Jack, can you hear me?' I shouted over the wind. I was deeply uncomfortable shaking this intellectual giant by the shoulders, but here was a fellow human in need. I was out of my depth, by a long way. There was a little blood on his head, but his eyes pinged open. 'I'm all right, I'm fine, absolutely fine, I'm sorry about this,' he rattled at lightning speed, coiled up and sprung upright, reaching for his briefcase. 'What happened?'

I pointed to the sign, now sliding and scraping along the ground a little way off, and then indicated the top of the scaffold.

'Yes, yes, I see, I see.' He spoke fast and intensely, just like he did in his lectures. He nodded, thanked me and sped off in the direction of the Newington Odeon while I tried to make sense of what had just happened.

I am certain he remembered none of this the next time he delivered a lecture on JM Barrie and *Peter Pan* to our class. There wasn't even a flicker of recognition when his gaze passed over me. I considered it a lucky escape. Even now, on a windy day in Scotland, I tend to look up rather than down, a life lesson taught to me by one of the most eminent literary scholars I have had the privilege to meet.

Daiva Ivanauskaitė – Lithuania

'I came to Scotland because of its storytelling tradition,' states Daiva Ivanauskaitė as if that was the most natural thing in the world. 'In Lithuania where I grew up, storytelling has very strict rules; it's about preserving our tales, showcasing dialect. Here the focus is much more on connecting with the audience, to entertain, perhaps to educate. I had heard there was a storytelling centre in Edinburgh, and that's why I came.'

Now a professional storyteller in demand, the Lithuanian is rightly proud of what she has brought to Scotland's cultural scene: a mix of traditional Lithuanian and Scottish tales and a celebration of global cultures and folklore. 'It's such a buzz when you are at a ceilidh or some other gig and you feel that connection with the audience, you watch them laugh, or cry – and you feel fantastic.'

Life in Scotland wasn't without its challenges. Finding an income was hard at first, and her first day of the six-month storytelling course wasn't a breeze either. 'I had been told: "10.00am. Don't be late." I didn't know how long my bus from Glasgow would take. It pulled into the bus station in Edinburgh at three minutes past ten and I still had to get to David Campbell's flat, my storytelling teacher. When I arrived, I rang the bell, frazzled. Silence. Then the door opened. "Yes? How can I help?" he asked. "I am so sorry, I am late!" I answered. He laughed and said, "You're a day early!" He simply invited me in, and the warmth of his hospitality blew me away. I spent all day there.'

The paradox is that Daiva finds it easier to do her job in English: 'In Lithuanian I am not so relaxed for some reason, always self-conscious, always doubting myself. I feel more free to tell my stories in English somehow.'

By now she is well connected and at home, with a Scottish husband and a young daughter. Nevertheless, she still feels like a foreigner. 'I am Lithuanian. When I open my mouth, anyone can hear I am not Scottish!' she laughs. 'We Lithuanians are very pro-EU and as a history and political science teacher in my old life, I am very interested in politics. To me, the EU is all about peace. About co-existence, about the ability to move around and experience a change of culture. I was very sad after the 2016 referendum and the choice the British people made. I asked myself: don't they believe in these values? Don't they see these benefits?' When Daiva arrived in Scotland in 2014, she stayed out of the independence debate. She felt she had no right to tell Scotland what to do. By now she is less reluctant to express her preference.

'People are always saying that Scotland is not capable, that we wouldn't manage on our own. If I could, I'd say to Scotland: You are totally ready, totally able. Totally worthy.'

7

Story

Half a capital and half a country town, the whole city leads a double existence; it has long trances of the one and flashes of the other; like the king of the Black Isles, it is half alive and half a monumental marble. –
Robert Louis Stevenson

BY WINTER, I was beginning to get the hang of this damp, foggy country. Scotland does atmosphere pretty well, doesn't it? Sitting upstairs in the red leather armchairs at Deacon Brodie's Tavern on the Royal Mile, I watched the cold mist crowd out the light of the streetlamps. I had been told that the real Deacon Brodie had likely inspired one of the books on my course reading list. That day, I had unearthed an old leather-bound copy of *The Strange Case of Dr Jekyll and Mr Hyde* in one of Edinburgh's West Port bookshops. No first edition, alas, but I was going to take no chances and stick to pencil.

That dark, rainy winter afternoon, I fell in love. Just like that. The atmosphere! Robert Louis Stevenson was a master at evoking a sense of menace, a sense of threat. This city peddled the past around every corner! Stevenson's Victorian setting did not seem so very far away from the cobbled streets I was looking down on right there. To most Scottish people, it is a classic they have heard about for as long as they can remember. To me, all of it was new. Despite its brevity, the text still strikes me as practically perfect: place (London) and characters (a range of Victorian gentlemen) blend into one another in a heady cocktail of story. And, in its own subtle way, there is magic, too: a scientific medical experiment turns the respectable and likeable Dr Jekyll into his evil alter-ego, Mr Hyde, a murderer and all-round despicable creature.

How? Stevenson does not concern himself with that question one bit.

Instead, he just gets on with the story, told from multiple viewpoints, revealing and resolving a plot that dances its way from beginning to end. The power of the potion to transform is dealt with in a single sentence about the liquid changing colour.

> The mixture, which was at first of a reddish hue, began [...] to brighten in colour, to effervesce audibly and to throw off small fumes of vapour. [...] The compound changed to a dark purple, which faded again more slowly to a watery green.

I can still hear Professor Campbell's voice as he all but hypnotised me, his gentle and melodious delivery weaving its very own magic on my mind. English was beginning to become my heart language, the one I dreamt in and the one which would come to me first. Stevenson's sentences sang: 'She had an evil face, smoothed by hypocrisy' and 'the fog still slept on the wing above the drowned city' – I was smitten, by the city of Edinburgh and by Scotland as story.

Of course, the book which comes to everyone's mind when Stevenson is mentioned is the ubiquitous *Treasure Island*. Back in Germany as a child, I had a manual projector with story slides of this book. Who could forget young Jim and his adversary, Long John Silver? Strangely, I took to this one the least, and always wondered why. It had it all, really: a fantastic villain, a child at the mercy of adult greed who has to find his own way in the world, plenty of sailing in dangerous waters, treasure and gunfire. Then I realised – I loved the Scotland which Stevenson created! I was much less fascinated with the South Seas or Southern France – give me the atmospheric, foggy world of a damp Scottish day instead, preferably in winter!

Decades later when I came across the real-life incident which inspired my own smuggling novella *Black Water*, I drew heavily on the Stevenson school of adventure-writing. The seizure of the smuggling ship *Rosamund* (in which Robert Burns participated as an exciseman) took place in February, by the sea, featuring smugglers and swordsmen, quicksand and cannon-fire, rising tides and a race against time. A child is at the mercy of adult greed and duty. Perhaps someday, someone will say: 'This story has Robert Louis Stevenson echoes' – there would be no higher compliment. In a pale imitation of the one who has gone before,

I'm trying for atmospheric, foggy, tense – a world full of intrigue, bravery and recklessness, too.

But aside from the storytelling, compelling though it may be, there is a universal truth which chimed with me in Stevenson's work: 'That man is not truly one but truly two.'

Stevenson's Jekyll may have been referring to the dual nature of good and evil in any soul, but as I was assimilating to life in Scotland, feeling at home in a culture which was not that of my birth, the words resonated with a different kind of truth. My identity need not be one thing and one thing only. Maybe I could be not truly one but truly two. Heck, maybe any one of us can be truly many, without guilt or betrayal. As our horizons expand, so can our souls, perhaps? In the wake of the Brexit referendum, I was to be drawn once more to the simple tale of *The Strange Case of Dr Jekyll and Mr Hyde*. Stevenson, the man, was complex: deeply rooted in the Edinburgh he called home, but fascinated by the world, hungry to travel and embrace the 'otherness' of new cultures. Of course, he too was a product of his time, as am I, as are all of us. But I wondered what he would have made of events which were to come in the 20th and 21st century, had he lived.

The fact that I found new nuances in a text I first read 25 years ago reinforced another power at work to me: the power of words, beyond time and circumstance. 2016 also marked another seismic change in my life: the publication of my first book. I was a professional writer. *Fir for Luck* was a Scottish historical tale about the clearances and was well received by readers, schools and critics alike, but I felt, in that year, simultaneously embraced and rejected. My nationality was no secret, but often, by assumption, I was described as a 'Scottish writer' in reviews. I did not go out of my way to deny it. In fact, what was Scottishness? In the discourse around the Brexit referendum, I also remember hearing the term 'Scottish by inclination' again, an offer which seemed almost too good to be true. You could be Scottish simply by wanting to be? Not truly one but truly two?

That sounded positively Stevensonian to me.

Petra Wetzel – Germany

Petra Wetzel was born in Bavaria but after more than two decades in Scotland she considers herself 'a proud Gerwegian'. She first fell in love with her adopted Scottish homeland on a school exchange. 'I was 13 and travelled to Stirling by bus with 50 other students. We pulled up at Stirling Castle, the sun was splitting the sky as it so often does and there was a piper playing. I'm not religious, but I remember thinking: *I've come home.*' In 1994 she returned to Scotland for good to study at the University of Glasgow.

The idea for WEST, her German-style brewery producing beers in strict accordance with traditional German Purity Law, has its roots in a visit from her father in those student days. He was unimpressed by what was being brewed locally at the time.

'I'm proud of what we've done: we have brought Scotland decent lager! And there is the venue too. Our Templeton Building beer hall on Glasgow Green may be authentic German style, but it's certainly not twee. It's becoming a Glasgow institution and all the taxi drivers know where it is!' She received an Honorary Doctorate for contributions to the Scottish economy from the University of Glasgow in 2015.

Many would argue that another of Petra's key contributions to Scotland is the investment fund, WEST Women, which she set up to give both financial and personal support to other budding female entrepreneurs. 'I think many women here are reluctant to take risks and that can be a problem. The most important thing is resilience.'

Petra Wetzel has never felt foreign in Scotland and feels very much part of the fabric here. In the early years she attended a dinner party where someone made a comment with a little innuendo. She quipped back: 'Oooh! Said the actress to the bishop!' which earned her a standing ovation from fellow guests – a social initiation.

After 22 years, Wetzel is now in the process of applying for British citizenship. 'I don't consider myself British at all, but what the hell,' she laughs. 'I need the passport to guarantee being able to travel. In my heart, I'd prefer a Scottish passport, but with my head I'm on the fence about independence. The truth is, I could never be a politician because I always say exactly what I think!' After the 2016 Brexit referendum, she turned on the TV and burst into tears: 'I was just thinking: *what have you done, people?*', she recalls.

She describes her European heritage as 'hugely important' to her and is proud to be German. 'My work ethic is definitely down to my parents who are grafters – the world owes me nothing! But saying that, I don't think I would have achieved what I did if I had stayed in Germany. I think the best thing I ever did was to combine two cultures in one life!'

Petra Wetzel has certainly come a long way since the famous *Dragons' Den* panel dismissed her pitch for a German-style brewery during the programme's first ever episode in 2004. Her outlook on life, and on Scotland, is sanguine: 'Life will throw shit at you. But Scotland doesn't gain anything from a chip on the shoulder about Westminster. Scotland has successes, inventions, explorers. Scots should be proud of their own achievements. Negativity about others is just such an unproductive feeling.'

8

Welcome!

Small cheer and great welcome makes a merry feast. – Shakespeare

UNIVERSITY DAYS BLENDED into one another. I was coping well with my courses, I had a great group of friends and I adored Edinburgh.

However, there was something which niggled, mostly subconsciously. I couldn't explain it or articulate it, but I was almost physically repelled by anything German. To most Scots, this may seem strange – expat Scots often turn into flag-waving, kilt-wearing dancers of jigs when abroad, reminiscing endlessly about their homeland. This was not the German way.

In fact, I'd go as far as to say that it was the opposite of the German way. My parents may only have been children during the Holocaust, but certainly in West Germany during the years of my schooling, the policy was to confront our nation's history head-on. 'Vergangenheits-bewältigung' was the buzzword – coping with one's past. The practical outworking of this was that history teaching comprised little other than Third Reich footage, harrowing and relentless. It was vital that history could never repeat itself. We had a responsibility to face it, and a responsibility to accept our new and humble place in the world. Scottish patriotism, as a result, sat a little uneasily with me. In fact, nationalism of any kind worries me even now – I am a product of my upbringing after all.

There was probably a little part of me that just wanted to fit in. I was studying English and Scottish Literature. Of course, I wanted to lose my German accent as far as I was able. Naturally, I didn't want to be the one who was marked out as different. And I was here to lose my accent and – if I'm honest – my German-ness, so I avoided other German students like the plague. Some of them huddled together anyway, and I was definitely not up for that.

But being an outsider bizarrely qualified me for the very thing I was trying to avoid – seeking out other incomers. At the time, there was an organisation comprised of all Edinburgh universities and colleges, the Edinburgh Christian Students' International Committee, ECSIC for short. 'Barbara, you know what it's like to be a foreigner. You should get involved in this!' several people suggested. It wasn't long before I was organising ceilidhs and coffee evenings for people like me – and despite all of this being a little counterintuitive at first, I actually enjoyed it. There were people from all over: America, Canada, Iran and Bulgaria, France, Germany, Poland and Spain. Attendees and volunteers mingled and made friends – and prepared for the big two weeks at the beginning of the next academic year: the ECSIC welcome.

I will never forget it. Waverley Station had lent us a portacabin for the fortnight. In the early '90s, many international students were arriving by train, and we were there to meet each and every one, with big signs saying things like, 'Are you an international student? Get your welcome pack here.' Often, we were the first friendly face at the end of a very long journey. We poured free coffee, called taxis, handed out maps and information booklets and arranged free meals and orientation trips. The shifts were long and intense, but many of my most enduring friendships which survive from that period were forged during the ECSIC welcome. We were a disparate bunch. My friend Jeremy was always an eccentric with his beard (long before beards became fashionable again), deerstalker hat and hunter's coat, holding up the sign beside an emptying train from King's Cross. We were in stitches when passers-by tossed pound coins at him, taking him for a beggar without bothering to read the sign.

On another day, we had hired a bus for a day trip to St Andrews, to give the new arrivals a flavour of Scotland before term commenced properly. Informal interest had been reasonable, but the huge coach we had already paid for seemed a foolish choice in that day's weather. The Scottish rain was unseasonably heavy and persistent. Despite that, more than 70 foreign students were already waiting. The young man I had danced with at the ceilidh, Rob, was in charge of the trip and his relief was palpable when he saw that the bus would be filled.

Soon, the lines between 'us' and 'them' blurred – was I us or was

I them? It didn't matter, and so I stopped concerning myself with the question. My life was too busy – there were places to explore and people to meet, books to read and lessons to learn, and I was ready to embrace it all.

Ironically, ECSIC is probably the reason I became adept at ceilidh dancing relatively quickly. Who doesn't love a bit of exercise, a bit of music and a laugh? On one occasion, our eccentric friend Jeremy was spinning a young lady from some country or other enthusiastically through the air. He may have been shouting with glee, but on landing, her scream turned into one of pain. She was clutching her leg.

As one, all the medical students in the room rushed forward to help.

Pretty much as one, they realised that none of them actually knew what to do, so they called an ambulance instead which amused the rest of us for some time.

I finally settled into a place of not needing a label. If someone called me 'the German girl' I did not resent it as much as I had at the beginning. Labels had simply ceased to be relevant, and I found that I liked it that way.

My weekly – and costly – phone call to my parents on a Sunday afternoon connected me with a country and a culture which seemed increasingly alien to me. They, in turn probably struggled to follow my enthusiastic rambles about life in Edinburgh. I had flown the nest and that was okay with both of us.

On visits home, however, I often found myself dismissing the German ways, idealising my new country and my new culture. 'This country has a National Health Service,' I boasted. 'Isn't that so much better than having to get health insurance? And people in Scotland are so much more informal than the Germans, I love it.'

But the truth of course, is that there are strengths and weaknesses to every system, every organisation, every country and every person, and deep down I probably knew it. Nevertheless, Scotland had my heart. I was glad of the four-year duration of my degree – I was young. At the time it felt as if I had all the time in the world!

Tim Visser – Netherlands

Netherlands-born rugby player Tim Visser, known as the 'The Flying Dutchman', scored 14 tries in 33 Tests after qualifying for Scotland through residency in 2012. The winger may have started his professional career at Newcastle after being discovered playing Sevens in the Netherlands, but he soon moved on to Edinburgh, where he was the leading try-scorer in the old Pro12 league for four successive seasons. He played over a hundred times for Edinburgh Rugby.

'I do feel part of Scotland and its culture. I think it's down to how I was received here as a foreign player, playing rugby for the national team. I felt at home almost straight away and accepted by the Scottish people who I played for.' He does recall his first encounter with *Flower of Scotland* with some embarrassment. 'We left the gates of Murrayfield to head to the airport for our flight to Australia for a tour. As we passed through Roseburn, Richie Gray stood up, walked to the front of the bus and grabbed the mike. 'Can we have Tim Visser for an anthem check please?' I got the first word wrong by starting with 'The flower of Scotland' and was booed back into my seat. This was followed by people like Geoff Cross deliberately passing me the wrong words if I asked for a sentence here or there which I'd forgotten. I ended up in front of the team on various buses, five times in total to get it right!'

His lowest point came when he broke his leg and couldn't play rugby for almost nine months, but he also cites the Brexit campaign in the run-up to the referendum in 2016. 'My strongest memory of that time is the continuous lying of the Leave campaign. That picture of the so-called Turkish immigrants trying to get into the EU was a real low point – the people in the picture were actually Syrians trying to escape their war-torn country.'

Following his retirement from rugby in 2019, Visser has continued to live and work in Edinburgh, but his Dutch heritage is very important to him. 'In my heart I'll always be Dutch. I wouldn't want to give up my Dutch passport, for example,' he says. 'I speak Dutch to my children and try and give them long summers back home around my family. I feel the need to pass on my language and culture.'

Visser's loyalty has long been to both Scotland and Holland. If

Scotland was a person, what would he tell her, I wonder? The Flying Dutchman is swift in his reply: 'Stay in the UK. The fact that the UK left the EU is a sad part of history already. Don't repeat the mistake!'

9

Over the Line

The birthplace of Valour, the country of Worth – Robert Burns

THERE WAS MUCH excitement in the spring of 1993: Ireland and Scotland were going to play each other at Murrayfield as part of the then Five Nations rugby tournament.

'We have to go!' Several of our friends hailed from Northern Ireland. We obsessively watched the other matches in the run-up.

However, something didn't sit right with me. I couldn't put my finger on it, apart from the fact that I was uneasy with the way the Scots, including my then-boyfriend, were supporting anyone but England.

'Ach it's all banter, that's all it is,' everyone responded when I challenged this. Football was the same – I had seen Scots buy Argentina shirts just to provoke the English. Why was this? I really wanted to know.

The answers varied. It was all to do with history, I was told by some. 'It's because of the English media,' others said, 'they always go on about 1966 and all that.' And yet I was uneasy with the sustained and targeted 'banter', which to my English friends felt like something else altogether. It didn't look like the feeling was reciprocated either. Did the English, on the whole, side against the Scots? No, they did not, as far as I could tell. Of course, if we do stereotype, each country has its nemesis, and these perceptions are rarely tidily reciprocal. After all, England will generally mark out the Germans as their arch-rivals in the sporting arena. And yet the Scottish strength of feeling against the English was unmatched by anything I had experienced elsewhere.

In fairness, I was no expert in patriotism. Things are different now, but my generation was, if anything, ashamed of being German. It was something to be kept, as my children would call it, *on the DL*. Scots, on the other hand were a liberty-loving nation of enthusiasts for their own country – something that felt more alien to me than the language or the culture.

'Listen, Barbara, you don't get it,' Rob said. 'We in Scotland – we lose, all the time. We expect it. England expect to win because they won in 1966, and that gets up our noses, as simple as that. It isn't hate. It really isn't.'

I was sceptical, but it seemed a little petty to get all wound up about my Scottish friends donning Argentinian face paint or splashing out on Brazilian football shirts whenever England faced such opposition. Did it matter? Does it matter now? If I'm honest, I still don't know. What I do know is that as a teacher, I can't be sanguine about the bullying a child faces when moving to Scotland from England, when they stand out for their 'posh' accent which is nothing but regional. I mind very much when a family of English incomers into Scotland can't attend a rugby match to support their home team without worrying about the hostility their youngsters will face. When only one side is laughing, it ceases to qualify as a joke, am I right?

As a German, I hadn't really come across rugby before. My brother-in-law had helpfully summed up the rules for me over the phone. 'You get 15 people in a team, and one ball. As far as I can tell, the teams more or less ignore the ball and beat each other up,' he laughed. 'Enjoy the match.'

In the rugby crowd on the day of that Scotland-Ireland match, England was silently present too, an invisible opponent. I don't think the rest of them even noticed it, but the sense of it followed me home, 'Proud Edward's Army' and 'Tae send them homeward tae think again'.

I had come to Scotland to analyse literature, after all. After the Second World War, only the third verse of our original German national anthem continued to be used, as the earlier version now had unfortunate and offensive connotations. The remaining words focus on unity, justice and freedom, the universal values we all hold dear. This unofficial Scottish anthem seemed to me to nurture an ancient grudge, a rousing hymn of defiance against a much-resented enemy. All around me, saltire-painted faces bellowed out the words (which I hadn't consciously heard until that day) with religious fervour. Later I learned that *Flower of Scotland* wasn't even an ancient tune – it was penned by Roy Williamson of the

Corries as a tribute to the Battle of Bannockburn. This was the '90s, for goodness' sake!

> O Flower of Scotland,
> When will we see
> Your like again,
> That fought and died for,
> Your wee bit Hill and Glen,
> And stood against him,
> Proud Edward's Army,
> And sent him homeward,
>   To think again.
>
> The Hills are bare now,
> And Autumn leaves
> Lie thick and still,
> O'er land that is lost now,
> Which those so dearly held,
> That stood against him,
> Proud Edward's Army,
> And sent him homeward,
>   To think again.
>
> Those days are past now,
> And in the past
> They must remain,
> But we can still rise now,
> And be the nation again,
> That stood against him,
> Proud Edward's Army,
> And sent him homeward,
>   To think again.

The very words were so adversarial, confrontational, imbibed with grudges and grumbles. I was uneasy.

I am not the only one who feels this way. One of Scotland's most famous rugby players called the song an embarrassing anti-English rant in an interview in 2009. Former British Lions captain, Finlay Calder, referred to *Flower of Scotland* as 'confrontational and antagonistic', suggesting that Scotland needed to 'grow up' in its rivalry with its southern neighbour. Capped 34 times for his country, he stated that being Scottish was rooted in fairness and openness. 'It's embarrassing, the lack of respect shown to English players. The anti-English stuff has got to stop. I think it's appalling the way we host our English competitors.' To him, *Flower of Scotland* was part of the problem, as well as the routine jeering of the English side at Scotland's national stadium at Murrayfield.

On that day, however, it was hard not to be swept along by the sheer passion of a stadium full of Scots, roaring rather than singing their hearts out. Relax, Barbara. This was no Nuremberg; this was no rally of hate. They wanted to win, and what was so wrong with that?

Allan had told me to enjoy the match – and enjoy it I did. I walked home as part of the victory crowd, talking fake-knowledgeably about Gavin Hastings, penalties, scrums and tries, humming *Flower of Scotland* under my breath and singing 'Tae think again' in the shower that night.

It was complicated.

Dr Eddy Graham – Ireland

Dr Eddy Graham has always felt that his Irishness was a bit of an advantage. 'People take to me easily – probably because I'm Irish,' he laughs. The lively weather and climate academic has repeatedly been voted most popular lecturer by his students at the University of the Highlands and Islands. On several occasions, BBC cameras rolled near the weather station in his garden on the Isle of Lewis. 'I am a self-confessed weather buff,' he admits. He feels at home here. 'There is a bit of affinity between the Scots and the Irish; their way of thinking and doing things is similar. For example, people are people and will make mistakes. They are both quite merciful, forgiving cultures. My Irish heritage is still huge for me – in the traditional rather than the religious sense. It's like James Joyce's short story *The Dead* which is all about our inability to shed our roots. But that doesn't mean we are insular – Ireland has always drawn its vitality from the European continent.'

Describing himself as an 'accepted outsider', he feels that it has been easier for him to tackle issues than for homegrown islanders, for example that of mental illness when he raised money for an eating disorder charity through a long-distance cycle. 'I am not a medic, so I am helpless to change anything practically – but I can raise funds by cycling and I can increase awareness, so that's what I'll do.'

Graham is an internationalist who trained south of the border in Reading before travelling widely, eventually settling in Switzerland where two of his children were born. The family moved permanently to Lewis, near his wife June's childhood home on the Isle of Skye, in 2009. Eddy's outgoing personality meant he soon made his mark, going by the name of 'Eddy Weather' and learning Gaelic. 'I used to think that I was no good at languages, but over the years I've become fluent in French and German and picked up a bit of Spanish and Italian too. I discovered that you *can* learn another language – all you need is immersion.'

When asked for his views on recent political events, the Irishman pulls no punches: 'Brexit was an act of national aggression – it still is. Brexit says: "We are unprepared to work with you on an equal level." And that has created a dangerous political situation. The same is happening in the USA. What's happening on both sides of the Atlantic is based on that same false delusion – that "we" are somehow superior. Those views have become so entrenched that it would take a real paradigm shift – and those tend to only come about through military intervention, which worries me.'

Eddy takes a deep breath before summarising: 'Ignorance is the danger. It's the main reason I am in education.'

So, what would Eddy Graham say to Scotland? He thinks for a moment and then laughs. 'I'd picture Scotland as a young female with her future ahead of her. I'd say: be independently minded and look after yourself. Don't forget where you've come from, beware of being manipulated. Be your own woman!'

10

The Open Door

Welcome, stranger. You shall be entertained as a guest among us. Afterward, when you have tasted dinner, you shall tell us what your need is.
— Homer

I HAD GROWN up in a house where there was room for the passers through. Friends from afar mingled with long-lost relatives from Brazil and Canada, France and Finland. Everyone was welcome – it was one of the things my parents did best until my father took ill.

In Scotland, I now found myself on the receiving end of hospitality. Moving out of halls so the space could be let for the month of the Easter holidays, I faced a choice: spend a lot of money on flying back to Germany (no low-cost airlines in those days!) or beg my local and not quite so local friends for a roof over my head and a corner for my clutter.

I was blown away by their generosity. Two of my weeks were going to be spent in Northern Ireland where I had never been. I was excited, but when I phoned my parents, the dampener came my way. 'Oh, Northern Ireland? We're not sure about you going there! There has been so much trouble in that place, Barbara. It's dangerous.' The limit of my exposure to Irish divisions and sectarianism had been Joan Lingard's *Across the Barricades* which I had read as a teenager and adored – one of the first novels I had read in English.

'It's not like that anymore, I think, Dad. My friends wouldn't invite me unless it was safe, and I've always wanted to go across the Irish Sea.'

'Well, you're an adult,' he said after a moment's silence – a phrase which commonly ended any conversation in which we disagreed, to avoid confrontation. I packed my bags.

The best part of visiting university pals at the end of term is that I didn't even have to take care of travel – I simply hitched a lift with my friend's parents who picked us up. I spent a lovely week sightseeing around Ballymena. In the second week, seven of us were going to get together and I couldn't wait! Somehow, we had access to a static caravan in Portrush and we were going to stay there as a group of friends. I must have inherited a little of my parents' anxious disposition after all, because I definitely looked over my shoulder more than I usually would, especially after a car backfired in the street. That moment showed up the clear distinction between those who had grown up during the Troubles and those who hadn't. My Northern Irish friends ducked into a crouch instinctively whereas the rest of us looked around, curious as to where the noise had come from.

Be that as it may, the trip did not quite work out as planned. The original idea was for four guys and three girls to spend the week together. Sharon called off early on. Fiona called off the day before. Before long, I found myself sharing a narrow caravan with four young gentlemen.

Everything was a logistical challenge. Someone in their wisdom decided that with partitions on either side, I should take the middle section, effectively sleeping on the dinner bench. That was fair enough – but if I needed the bathroom, I had to disturb Adrian and Rob. If I wanted to leave the caravan, I had to disturb Chris and Dickie. And if I wanted to change, I was entirely relying on the goodwill on both sides, hoping that neither side would accidentally twitch the precariously fixed curtains aside. It felt like the proverbial white-knuckle ride.

During that holiday I realised that, for all my fondness for everyone there – these were some of my closest friends – I was still different. An evening was spent reminiscing about childhood TV programmes, for example. Predictably I laughed along, but I couldn't share the memories, just as they would have given me blank stares if I had begun to sing theme tunes to *Die Biene Maja* or *Wiki der Wikinger*. Irish and Scottish friends shared memories which I could not. On the other hand, I was able to contribute handily to an entertaining discussion about animal noises. If you can believe it, that was the first time I had given serious thought to what noise a cockerel made. 'Cock-a-doodle-doo' seemed utterly ridiculous to me. Everyone knew that a cockerel's call was 'kikeriki' didn't they? We laughed a lot that night.

The common perception is of course that Germans do not have a sense of humour. The truth is that it did take some getting used to the humour in my adopted culture. Why was it that laughter inevitably followed when one good friend 'slagged another off'? When Scots and Irish people like someone, they insult each other with enthusiasm. It was not something I had come across in my high school English classes, unsurprisingly. Why would anyone deliberately ridicule another, or say the opposite of what is meant as a mark of affection? Make their friends look ridiculous? On purpose? I was baffled. This kind of humour did not come easily to me. Neither did the machine gun exchange of witticisms which characterised most of this holiday – this wasn't my first language and I struggled to keep up. My Irish friend Chris came to the rescue. 'Barbara, if people like you, and if people care about you, they will have banter. They will slag you off, mercilessly. It means they like you. They are comfortable around you. They expect you to do it back to them.'

I thought about this for a moment. If it was a compliment to be on the receiving end of what they called 'the craic', I should be flattered and proud, not hurt and doubtful. Granted, my first few forays into the world of this strange new humour were a bit hit-and-miss, but I was going to get the hang of it, and if it was the last thing I did!

My visual memories of the week on the Northern Irish coast consist of wide sky, the incredible scale of the Giant's Causeway and laughter, so much laughter. But the strongest memory is of an utterly domestic moment.

Spring in Northern Ireland is no different from Scotland, really: characterised by rain and wind, and by the absence of the sunshine to which we somehow feel entitled during holidays. Caravan nights were exceptionally cold.

Every night we filled up our respective hot water bottles from the tiny kettle in the caravan kitchen. It was the ritual before the pulling of the two dividing curtains across, granting me my slither of privacy.

That night, I woke up shivering. A moment of confusion followed. What was happening? Why was everything sticking to me? Was I ill?

The reason was simple – the seal of the hot water bottle had given way and my night clothes, sleeping bag and padded bench were oozing water. I jumped up with a cry, but all I heard from either side were the young-men snores of warmth and comfort.

I mumbled a few unusually colourful words under my breath and cast around in the dark, but no – all spare blankets were in use as extra layers over the boys on either side. There wasn't even a tablecloth. Some of the deluge had even leaked into my bag which had been leaning against the bench. I found the driest of the T-shirts within and pulled it over my head. Discarding sleeping bag and pillow, I pulled on my dirty jeans from the day before and spread a small hand towel over my torso by way of a blanket. It was a woeful night. My only comfort was the self-righteous thought of how considerate I was being, not waking my friends and demanding assistance.

That I was a little grumpy the following morning as my well rested companions emerged is an understatement. Crouching outside and wringing my bedding out, Chris joined me and put a hand on my shoulder. 'You know, Babs, it could have been worse. So much worse.'

'How?' I replied monosyllabically.

'Well… it could have been me!' he laughed, before jumping up and joining the lads.

Now, that was the least funny thing I had ever heard.

I didn't even have the energy to punch him!

Gio Benedetti – Italy

Innovator, millionaire businessman, serial entrepreneur – whichever way you choose to describe Tuscany-born Gio Benedetti, his story with Scotland is remarkable. The young Benedetti's work ethic was evident from the beginning when his ambitious working-class parents sent him to Scotland on his own, aged only ten. He spoke no English. 'I must have been a bad boy for my parents to send me,' he laughs, but the young Giovanni was placed with his uncle in Irvine to be educated. He earned his keep by working in the family café every day after school. School was a culture shock: 'I had come from Italy, so I thought the whole world was Catholic! There was a wall between my Catholic school and the Protestant one beside it. We used to throw snowballs across it. Sometimes maybe a brick inside the snowball!'

Joking aside, Benedetti's contribution to the Scottish and UK economy is considerable: he has started companies and employed thousands of people in a spirit of constant innovation and entrepreneurship, which he also sought to pass on to others. As a founding member of The Prince's Trust Scotland and through his involvement in one of their programmes, Youth Business Scotland, he has helped hundreds of young hopefuls achieve their ambitions.

Benedetti began his career in garment cleaning, the first business he bought, aged only 18. Soon he was cleaning gloves and garments for Ford, Nissan, Jaguar, Vauxhall and Rover. Diversification was always his trademark: he developed an innovative clingfilm dispenser and sold first aid kits for use in industrial settings. Other products included eco-handle shopping bags, cradle-safe baby monitors and ampoule openers for medical use, to name but a few. Perhaps most impressive is the innovator's Airglove device which Mr Benedetti designed under his company, Green Cross Medico, to ease the often traumatic process of achieving venous access – the product is already in use in hospitals across the UK. It seems that, even now, he has no appetite for retirement.

A ferocious work ethic clearly runs in the family: Gio Benedetti is the father of virtuoso violinist and Grammy winner Nicola Benedetti, with his daughter Stephanie also a successful musician.

Despite his many decades in Scotland, Benedetti retains his Italian passport – and his strong Italian accent. He describes himself as 'neutral' on Brexit but feels strongly about Scottish independence: 'This separation scenario is not right! I say to Scotland: love England!'

But he has nothing but love and positivity for his adopted homeland. 'I love Scotland. I feel Scottish,' he declares confidently. 'Everything I've got, Scotland has given me.'

SCOTTISH BY INCLINATION

II

Work

No bees, no honey; no work, no money. – traditional proverb

I HAD MADE a deal with my parents: if I was to study abroad, I would receive the same level of financial support from them as my sisters had. I soon discovered that this did not only mean I would have to live frugally and say no to many of the balls and parties on the university's social calendar. No, if I wanted to eat and socialise and travel back to see my folks, I would have to work.

A strong work ethic was inherent in my upbringing. As soon as I was old enough to make any money at all, pocket money allowance stopped. I walked neighbours' dogs and tutored younger pupils in subjects I was good at – mainly English. I vividly remember my first solo trip to the UK as a teenager. It was solely funded by tutoring cash and, even now, no other achievement in my life compares with what that felt like.

Now I needed a way of making money that would not interfere with my studies, or my many evening commitments courtesy of a number of societies at university. One of the ventures I pursued was translation. An ambitious fourth year student called Justin had advertised for help with translation projects. I was gobsmacked at the rewards on offer – *ker-ching!* But once I was in charge of translating a chemical processing manual, I quickly fell out of love with translation: too many scientific terms, too much complexity, too little will to live. I completed the project, took the money and ran a mile.

Signing up with an employment agency seemed like a logical next step. After all, I had waitressing experience from my two Blackpool restaurant summers. How hard could it be?

But like most people on their books, I was only contacted sporadically.

My first and most memorable waitressing gig was a reception at the iconic Edinburgh City Chambers where I was astonished by the rude behaviour of some of the attendees towards us waiting staff. Weaving through packed crowds of suits with trays of drinks or canapés, we were either invisible or on the receiving end of over-familiarities we had not invited. This kind of waitressing was not for me, I thought. I lacked the necessary eyes in the back of my head.

In any case, the income from the agency wasn't regular enough. Walking along the Royal Mile, I spotted a small handwritten note in the window of a tiny newsagent's shop, on the corner with Jeffrey Street and opposite the World's End pub. 'Part-time help needed. Apply within.'

It was ideal work for me. In the middle of the city centre, but very much part of the largely working-class community of old Edinburgh, I adored the bustle of the shop and would spend the next three years working there very happily. A typical Saturday or Wednesday shift would see me delivering the *Edinburgh Evening News* to the nearby sheltered housing complex as well as working behind the till. I was friendly with many of the residents there, but my favourite was the then octogenarian daughter of an Argentinian diplomat whose flat was decorated with glamorous photographs of her, posing with famous faces of decades gone by. I called her Susannah. I couldn't remember her second name in any case, and her English was terrible. I remember her glee when we discovered that not only was I her papergirl, but we also attended the same church. In fairness, Susannah attended every church in the vicinity, including daily Mass at the nearby cathedral.

With the shop located on the Royal Mile, we rarely missed an occasion. Behind the till, I was ideally positioned to see Prince Charles ride by in a royal carriage as bystanders jeered, 'Where's Camilla then?' It was the immediate aftermath of Diana's infamous interview with Martin Bashir: 'There were three of us in the marriage, so it was a bit crowded.'

But dealing with tourists never failed to entertain. It was *them*, and it was *us*. Despite my German passport, I was declared part of the *us*. A little odd, but lovely. Tony, my boss, hailed from England. He was hardworking and kind, as was his wife Evelyn whom I remember for her incredible warmth towards me.

One day a visitor entered the shop and, in and in broken English, asked for, 'Five postcards please.' I showed her the selection.

'Stamps for Italy?' she gestured.

I sold her stamps and airmail stickers. The shop was filling up, but she borrowed my pen and stood in the corner to write her cards, leaning on the freezer chest. Once complete, she laboriously licked her stamps, fixed them on and made to leave.

'Where?' she asked, waving the fistful of correspondence.

'Post box. Red box. Just there.' I gestured through the window to indicate the bright red Royal Mail postbox.

'For letter?' she asked.

'For postcards and letters yes.' I answered, nodding and pointing again at the red box.

'Letter. Okay. I go,' she declared, and the doorbell rang out with her exit as I bent down to retrieve a packet of cigarettes for one of our regulars. But then something across the road caught my eye. The tourist had walked right past the bright red Royal Mail postbox and, in one elegant movement, slid her clutch of cards into the bin.

'Excuse me! Can I pay for those now?' The irritated voice of the customer in front of me catapulted me back into the present, and the next time I looked, the lady in question had been swallowed up by the throng of visitors to the city.

It was only on my way home that I investigated a little more closely and discovered that on the grey bin there was a large inscription: LITTER. I tried to see if I could retrieve the cards, but they were buried deep. I'm not proud of it, but I walked away.

Tony laughed about it for a week. I couldn't help laughing along too, despite the fact that my mirth was lined with guilt.

The ignorance of the foreigner – that could have been me.

A couple of years later, Tony and Evelyn were preparing to sell the shop, just as I was getting ready for my wedding. I explained about the German tradition of a cake reception in the afternoon, but the kitchen in my shared flat was woefully inadequate – definitely not the place to bake cakes for more than a hundred hungry students.

'Do it in mine,' Evelyn said simply. And so it was that I took a bus to Liberton, entered a house I had never visited before with a giant backpack full of flour, sugar, eggs and apples in order to bake a dozen cakes, the day before my wedding. I will never forget their kindness to their Saturday girl and I often wonder what became of them. If anyone knows, I'd love you to tell me.

Another job I took on during my student years was in a card shop on Nicolson Street where I worked for a summer. It was a small affair with no more than two members of staff on shift at any one time – a supervisor and a minion. To be clear, I was the minion. My boss was also new into post: a young woman from Northern Ireland, only a few years older than me. She made me memorise all the different wedding anniversaries until they were firmly lodged in my memory, and we got on well, but I was still surprised when she invited 'Barbara and Partner' to her wedding. My first Scottish wedding! I was beyond excited. The invitation stated we should make our way to the Hydro Hotel. Scrubbed up and clad in our glad rags, Rob and I jumped on a bus and headed south.

Weddings can be tricky, especially when you don't know anyone at all except for the bride. She, as you may imagine, was otherwise occupied. Apart from a quick hug and a 'so, so glad you could make it' I saw nothing of her but a veil blowing in the wind and a photographer's back. Rob and I milled around, sipping our drinks and talking to each other. I am fairly sociable but even I was finding it a little awkward. It was Rob's idea to shuffle surreptitiously towards a group of bystanders and on the count of three, to laugh loudly. Invariably that attracted their attention and we shrugged in a 'you had to be there' sort of way before introducing ourselves. And that, believe it or not, is how I met the great poet Edwin Morgan. To this day I have no idea what his connection to the bride or groom was. A glamorous lady initiated the conversation and introduced herself. The predictable questions followed.

'I work with Kirsten,' I chimed in with my answers. 'I'm Barbara, a student at Edinburgh University. This is my boyfriend Rob.'

Interest was feigned. What were we studying?

Rob answered first and the discussion revolved around medicine for a minute. 'This year I'm doing Scottish Literature and English Language,' I added.

'Oh, my friend here is a poet. You might have heard of him. He is quite well known.'

The quiet man beside her made self-deprecating gestures.

'Barbara, this is Edwin Morgan.'

The floor began to sway. He smiled at me, his eyes calm pools of vague interest.

I had his entire published works on my shelf. I had sat through many lectures and tutorials on his poems, taken copious notes. And yet here I stood, without a single intelligent thought in my head. I scrambled wildly, but no, none would form either. I babbled some nondescript nonsense for an excruciating eternity and eventually found a reason to run. And there, ladies and gentlemen, is the greatest regret of my professional writing life. I met a genuine legend of words, and threw an opportunity of a lifetime away. On the bus back to Edinburgh, I thought of countless articulate statements and millions of erudite observations. I thought of witty ways I could have woven references to his poems into conversation. Did he remember me after a couple more drinks?

I sincerely hope not.

I dread the thought of what his razor-sharp observation might have made of me.

Julija Pustovrh – Slovenia

Inspired by nature. Made in Scotland. So goes the slogan which introduces the world to Emporium Julium, Slovenian-born Julija Pustovrh's work. The former landscape architect describes herself as a designer at heart; she makes unique organic ceramics which capture the aesthetic philosophy behind her work. Julija's journey to Scotland is not unusual: 'I arrived in Edinburgh in 2011 to live and study here, and to be with my partner who is also Slovenian. He had come to study at the University of Aberdeen two years before. It is difficult to describe how I feel after all these years living here. I think in terms of identity, I feel somewhere in between the two countries. Scotland is my home now, but sometimes I do feel like a foreigner. It really depends on the situation, and how you feel changes over time.'

Julija's work is rustic, distinctive and completely at home in the wild Scottish landscape from which she draws so much inspiration. 'I do think that my artwork and my ceramics have caused me to get more entangled with Scottish landscapes and nature, and thus I am giving back to Scottish society. My ongoing Sandscape Collection is made with Scottish sand that I collect in remote coastal areas. I mix it with clay and produce tableware that people can then use – bringing the beautiful nature of Scotland into our homes.'

She is coy about giving too much away but cherishes memories of her adopted homeland. 'Scotland is often a bit mysterious so I will keep my most moving memory here a mystery too,' she laughs. 'It's safe to say, it involves an old tradition, a stunning place and the love of my life. But there have been many high points!' She lists the astonishing response to her latest exhibition, swimming in the clear turquoise sea on the Isles of Lewis and Harris and a relaxed day spent walking on North Ronaldsay, to name but a few. 'You can really feel the remoteness of these places and the calmness takes over. Everything else takes the back seat for that moment.'

Julija remembers being with friends and colleagues at the time of the Brexit referendum and feeling sad and disappointed at the results of the vote. 'At the same time, I also felt there was hope, being in Scotland as opposed to down south. We still felt accepted and welcomed.'

Her ceramics may echo Scotland's landscape and wilderness, but her outlook on life and art is far from parochial: 'My Slovenian history is very important to me, and even more so after Brexit. I feel like I am, and we all are, a part of Europe as a whole. We should embrace it, connect, help each other and share – not put up borders and restrictions.'

12

Places

There is a time and place for everything. – traditional proverb

GRADUALLY, I BEGAN to make memories of my own. Of course, Edinburgh was where it started for me. The university and Pollock Halls at the foot of Arthur's Seat, student flats in Marchmont, Causewayside and Polmont, libraries and favourite cafés. Of those, my go-to was a small affair on Victoria Street called Kinnell's. Everything, simply everything, about that café appealed to me. Healthy vegetarian options, dark mismatched wooden furniture, tartan cloth instead of wallpaper. Somehow, it never felt twee to me at all. Up the black metal spiral staircase, there was a large table right by the window on the first floor and we would hover nearby and hog it as soon as its previous occupants left. As everyone's lectures for the day finished, they would show up and add themselves to our number, squeezing onto the bench or pulling up extra chairs. Permeating through the space was the smell of freshly ground coffee. The café is closed now and the last time I checked it had been converted into a restaurant, but I cannot walk past the doorway without remembering. I hear echoes of laughter, of my first flirtatious exchanges with Rob, or the relay of complaints about lectures and workload with each new arrival. It was here in Kinnell's that I first came across Charles Rennie Mackintosh's designs, too – all signage and menus were paying homage to him. All these things about Scotland to discover! I was hungry for new impressions and Scotland's larder was well stocked.

Then there were the dark red buses. Who had ever heard of needing the correct change? This was definitely not the German way! I ventured as far as Cramond and the Pentlands. Being part of a church also unlocked Edinburgh suburbia as we students were often invited back for Sunday lunch.

One such invitation took us to the house of our minister at the time, a passionate white-haired, wiry Welsh preacher called Brian who regularly pounded the pavements of Marchmont jogging, accompanied by his pet dog Monty. His wife was quietly kind. I was drawn to their international perspective – they had spent many years living in Belgium and made frequent and fond reference to mainland Europe.

We sat through the obligatory Sunday roast, making polite conversation. There were three of us invited on that day: my boyfriend Rob, an American exchange student and myself. After lunch, Rob offered to help make coffee and he and Brian disappeared into the kitchen.

Talking to only the American was even harder, especially because it sounded as if we were missing some sort of party in the kitchen. However, soon they emerged with a cafetiere and heated milk for the coffee – an absolute luxury. I was so taken with it that I barely paid attention when the plate of biscuits was passed round. I took one.

'These only come out for really special visitors,' enthused the old man. 'Belgian speciality. They take some getting used to but now they're my favourite!'

The coffee was excellent. I must say, I was less enamoured with the Belgian biscuits which, to me, seemed distinctly hard and bordering on odd in taste. At least they were small – I'd get through it, I supposed. The eager man of the cloth passed me the plate again. 'Good eh?'

With difficulty, I gulped down the rest of my biscuit, washing it down with half a mug of coffee. The American, from what I could see, was grimacing a little too.

I declined politely. 'I'll pass, thanks. But it was good to try them.'

'Acquired taste, huh?'

'Perhaps.'

Only then did I notice that Rob's silent giggles were rocking the sofa. I caught his eye, and it was over. Brian and Rob were what the Scots called 'in stitches'. The door clicked open and the minister's wife came into the living room and took in the scene. Her eyes widened at the sight of the plate of biscuits. 'Oh Brian, you've done it AGAIN!'

The two culprits continued to laugh as she slid the biscuits to the ground where Monty the dog swiftly gobbled them up. 'Feeding the guests dog biscuits! Really, Brian!'

After a momentary gagging reflex, I couldn't help but join into the laughter – still the loveliest thing about the sense of humour here. It's perfectly acceptable, even encouraged to laugh at yourself. I will always love that.

Looking back, the flipping biscuits were bone-shaped! How could I not have noticed? Whenever I think of it, I still cringe. What an idiot I was.

Which places became dear to me in my first few years in Scotland depended entirely on their accessibility by public transport. Peebles, St Andrews and North Berwick became regular haunts, as did South Queensferry where the imposing Forth Rail Bridge took my breath away. The exception was the Isle of Iona which I had wanted to see ever since taking an outside course in Celtic Civilisation. Getting there was tricky, but its history had fascinated me for years. The thought that the Celts, as we call them today, had their origins in southern Europe really intrigued me. Everyone is an immigrant if you look closely enough. I hatched a plan to go with three Northern Irish friends. Two tents, a combination of buses and ferries, no problem.

The trip was bathed in sunshine and the hand of the past lay heavily on my shoulder as I prayed in the place where St Columba is said to have first arrived more than a thousand years ago. I knew that the iconic Celtic cross by the abbey was a replica, but in the crypt, there were fragments of original stonework. Whose were the hands which had chiselled these patterns? Where had they hailed from? Where would they meet their end? In a Viking raid? On a coracle, swept out to sea by the surf?

The island had an atmosphere, make no mistake. In the past I had been sceptical about the idea of 'thin' places, where the physical and the eternal are separated only by the thinnest of veils, but I wasn't so sure now. I had felt the same, to some extent, standing on the Giant's Causeway.

When we had to pass a few hours due to a bus delay, I took a wander along the coast at sunset. The evening clouds melted into a swirl of colours and I was alerted to a strange sound. There were seals in the water, I thought. Many.

The sight of that colony of seals, splashing on the surface of the sea and singing their songs into the evening breeze on that day will be lodged in my memory until the day I die. There was something surreal about it, something magical. I sometimes wonder if I dreamt it all. That weekend sealed a lifetime love of the islands, of Celtic Christianity and of stone carvings.

Over the years, other places became special: places I had chosen to visit and places I stumbled upon, some places which inspired books of mine. I found new cafés and cubbyholes, valleys and vistas. I explored with an intensity I probably never had in Germany. Why?

Because there, essentially, I had been a child. Here, I was an adult with agency – my choices were mine and mine alone.

This amazing new country was my oyster.

Silviya Mihaylova – Bulgaria

'How I came to Scotland? That's a long story!' begins Bulgarian pianist Silviya Mihaylova.

'I was living in Bulgaria and planning to study music somewhere in Eastern Europe. In 2005 I came to visit my brother in Glasgow, just as a tourist, and he took me to a concert, a piano and cello performance at the concert hall. The pianist was a Professor Fali Pavri. I was completely blown away. Honestly, it was probably the most impactful concert I have ever attended, pure magic. Afterwards my brother encouraged me to go backstage and speak to the great pianist. I was terrified but I introduced myself to him. "Who are you?" the professor asked. I explained that I was studying piano in Bulgaria. "Play for me," he told me. I played some Chopin. "Apply to the Royal Scottish Academy of Music and Drama," he concluded. "I'd love to teach you." And that was that. I was 16 years old.'

Silviya is now the pianist for Sound Collective Scotland and the accompanist for the Glasgow Philharmonic Male Voice Choir. Following a Bachelor and a Master's degree in piano performance from the Academy, now called the Royal Conservatoire of Scotland, she balances performance and lecturing at her alma mater with motherhood. 'I love what I am part of: inspiring and helping the next generation of musicians and music lovers.'

She fondly recalls her involvement in Live Music Now Scotland, a charity bringing classical music to places where it is rarely performed and presenting emerging professional musicians with performance opportunities. 'I've performed in schools, care homes and in remote rural communities. I remember giving a concert in Shetland. After the programme, a young girl and her family hung back. I wondered why they weren't leaving. When I went over, the girl shyly said: "When I grow up, I want to be you." That really touched me – the power of music.'

On another occasion she played in a home for patients with dementia. A very elderly lady began to cry during Silviya's rendition of *Au Clair de la Lune*. 'I was horrified that I had upset her and rushed to speak to her. "No," the woman answered. "This was my husband's favourite piece of music. While you were playing it, I was with him again."' Borders and time became unimportant: a Bulgarian musician, a French tune and a Scottish lady's memories, merged through music.

By contrast, the 2016 referendum was Silviya's lowest point in Scotland. 'The beauty of being a musician is the international community you become part of. Voting to come out of that community, isolating ourselves, just felt like such a backward view. I met a French-speaking friend for coffee the morning after the referendum and we made such an effort to speak in English, and without an accent. It was probably irrational, but we were actually afraid to speak our own language. It didn't work. 'Are you two from Scotland?' the waitress asked us. We reluctantly admitted that we weren't. "Good!" the waitress said decidedly. "We want you to stay!"'

Despite widespread support like this, there are moments of frustration. 'We foreigners are all super-polite and don't question anything, but I have a baby now. She is British. I've invested so much in this country and yet I am not. It makes no sense. How can she be more British than I am?'

13

I Do

What's in a name? – Shakespeare

IT HAD HAPPENED. I was engaged! Just like that.

In Germany, all of this happens very differently – there is a procedure. A nervous young man on one knee is not the big thing – most Germans don't even remember the date of popping the question. No, an engagement is handled like a wedding day there – something one schedules, fits into the diary and invites guests to. My mind was officially blown: here in Scotland, you could answer a simple question in the affirmative and, *ta-dah*, you were engaged. It was crazy!

And so the preparations began. As both of us were still students, our wedding probably went off a bit differently to most people's. We had no money, for a start. But that wasn't a huge obstacle. Who says a wedding dress had to be new? Who says you have to celebrate at a hotel? Who says?

Having hosted the obligatory engagement party in Germany, complete with ceilidh dancing (which the Germans loved!), we returned to Scotland to resume our studies – and to plan a wedding. Gosh, it seemed like such an adult thing to do. If I'm honest, there were times when I felt like I was pretending the whole thing. At 21, I didn't feel old enough to tackle an event of this magnitude and significance, not remotely! Oddly enough, I never had doubts about getting married itself – just the logistics. Youth is a wonderful thing: you may feel daunted, but to some extent you are convinced that you're invincible too. If we put our minds to it, of course we could do it!

There were all sorts of tricky adult things to get our heads around. My birth certificate, for example, needed to be translated and verified in order for us to apply for a marriage licence. No problem – I simply wandered up to the floor in the David Hume Tower where my English Language lecturer Heinz Giegerich had his office. He was talking to a couple of colleagues, sitting on rather than at his desk and laughing as I knocked onto the open door.

'Could you translate my birth certificate and certify it in some way? It's for official business. I'm getting married.'

He smiled. There were appreciative, well-wishing kind of comments from the others. He took a look at the sheet of paper in my hand. 'I will see what I can do,' he said before calling on the departmental secretary.

I walked out with a carefully typed, English-language edition of my birth certificate, verified by the signature of one Prof. Dr. Giegerich and the official stamp of the University of Edinburgh. One down, a hundred tasks to go.

We found a community hall in South Queensferry, one of our favourite places to visit. It would do well for the low-key reception we had planned, despite my sister's longing look at the Balmoral's iconic silhouette. But my favourite afternoon in the run-up to the big day was a shopping trip with Rob's young aunt, Jackie. There were so many charity shops on the stretch along South Clerk Street and Nicholson Street – we were bound to strike lucky. I had never had any notion of finding *the perfect dress*. I simply wanted to find *a dress*, one I liked and could afford. We entered the first shop. 'Do you have any wedding dresses?'

The volunteer behind the counter stared me up and down, did the same to Jackie and shook her head. By the time we got to the fifth and sixth shop, my smile was beginning to wear thin. We had seen one or two, but nothing either of us liked, and certainly none that would have fitted me. I was a size 12, fairly standard for a young woman of marrying age. Why was this so difficult?

We entered a large shop with high hopes. I wheeled out the most charming smile I could muster. 'Do you have any wedding dresses?'

The young woman rang a bell to ask her manager.

'We do...' the older woman said when she arrived. 'But they are a bit big for the shop floor and we tend to save them up for early spring, you know? Beginning of wedding season.'

I was about to turn on my heels as I had done six times before, but she held me back. 'You could always look at them downstairs in our storage area. If you don't mind.'

Jackie and I exchanged a glance. *The belly of the beast? Yes please.* To this day, I adore the thrill of a treasure hunt in a second-hand shop. The cellar was a windowless room with endless hangers of garments, a muted mosaic of fraying fabric in the soulless strip light. And there it was – a whole length of rail with nothing but wedding dresses.

I approached with awe as the manager hovered. I don't know what she was worried about. It's not like I could have made off with a gown of this size rolled beneath my jumper. But my thoughts were otherwise occupied. The first bright white satin affair was swiftly dismissed. I could tolerate puff sleeves, but not balloon-ish degrees of puff. As I slid dress by dress along the steel, I became aware of the palette. 'Hey Jackie – aren't wedding dresses supposed to be white? Look at this one? Kind of cream-coloured.'

Jackie took a step towards me. 'Oh, look at that! It's ivory. Lots of people go for ivory.'

They didn't where I came from.

But as I ran my fingers carefully over the lace, the buttons and the pearly droplets on the sleeves, I realised that something about this dress was different.

'Come here; look at this.' I beckoned her close and whispered, just audible under my breath.' It's got a really nice feel.'

She searched for the label and gave a sharp intake of breath. 'It's pure silk! I can't believe it's pure silk for £50.' She spoke almost silently, her lips barely parting. I unhooked the hanger and held the dress up to the manager, feigning nonchalance.

'May I try this one on please?'

It fitted. Of course it did; it was meant to be. It may not have been the dress of my dreams, but it was good quality, pretty and it had history. I loved that.

Several months before the wedding, we began to think about decorations. We had plenty of friends and were still heavily involved in the international student welcome committee. It made sense to host a number of open evenings. 'Hey friends,' we put on a little card we handed out to everybody we knew. 'We're getting married. We can't possibly make all the decorations for the wedding alone. Come round to Rob's flat on any Thursday evening and help us. We will ply you with plenty of tea.'

And they came: PhD students from India were tying miniature bows for the orders of service with French exchange students. Literature buddies joined medics to knead salt dough into candlesticks for the tables. Two or three fashioned large paper knots and bows out of decorative paper which were in turn glued onto prepared pound-shop trellises to fill the large walls of the Rosebery Hall. Folding of invitations, cutting of seating plans, assembly of dried flowers – you name it, we tackled it together. The beauty of getting married as students was that we could tear up the rule book. We weren't in charge of delivering the perfect celebration on a plate for our friends. We needed them, and they knew it.

As expected, there was much discussion of wedding traditions in different countries, too, with candlelight and laughter in abundance. But I had no doubt about it now: I wasn't just marrying a man – I was marrying a country. And I was bringing my own with me.

The wedding day itself went by in a blur. I remember getting stuck in traffic on George IV Bridge and having to walk down the Royal Mile in my wedding dress so I wouldn't be late. Rob had joked that he wouldn't hang around if I was delayed, but he needn't have worried – I think most Germans are hard-wired for punctuality, and my family in particular would rather die than be late for anything at all. During the bilingual service in our church, the minister of dog-biscuit-fame absentmindedly introduced us to the congregation as Mr and Mrs Haas, my maiden name, only for the entire crowd to correct him aloud. That was followed by a cake reception in which my dozen cakes, baked in the newsagent's kitchen, took pride of place. The wedding photographer was particularly meddlesome, I recall. In the evening at South Queensferry, the reception was split into ceilidh dancing (the Scottish way) and a variety show put on by wedding guests (the German way). And, just like that, I had become Mrs Henderson.

The name was going to prove handy for what I was planning to do next with my life. I had come round to the idea of teaching English – which might just be the sort of job in which parents of pupils might prefer a native speaker. At least my name wouldn't give me away. The German part of my identity had become invisible, camouflaged and only detectable if you looked for it.

To be honest, I kind of liked it that way.

Dr Ksenija Horvat – Croatia

'I've felt foreign all my life.' It is a stark response to my question whether the Croatian-born Media Communication and Performing Arts lecturer still feels foreign in Scotland.

She explains: 'As a working-class ethnic Croatian, I always felt foreign in communist Yugoslavia. That sense of not belonging has stayed with me. If anything, I feel more at home here in Scotland than I ever have anywhere else. I have come to realise that home is where the people you care for are.'

During the civil war, Horvat worked for the Croatian government until she could be sure that her parents and family were safe. Only then did she seek to pursue her own passion: drama – first by moving to Ireland to study for a Master's degree in Irish theatre and then on to Edinburgh for her PhD. The young academic stayed with local families, a choice she credits with helping her become familiar with Scots and their culture. 'There are a lot of similarities to Croatia in the community where I live here in Edinburgh, a mix of students and working-class families. We may have different traditions, but many of our values are the same – and these values are still very much alive. It's this sense of community, trying to resurrect itself.'

She recalls the mornings after both referenda, the independence referendum in 2014 and the Brexit vote in 2016. 'Both times, I knew instinctively which way it had gone. I live in a part of Edinburgh where people like to celebrate – for example winning at football. Generally, there is always chatting in the street, and any excuse for fireworks! On those mornings though, there was nothing but an eerie silence. Things were not as they should be. It just felt desolate. That sort of silence chills you to the bone; you can't replicate that.'

Being an immigrant in Scotland has not always been easy, she allows: 'But the challenges I have faced are not specific to Scotland – I may have faced them anywhere in the world. Nevertheless, the truth is, as a foreigner, you continuously have to prove yourself, prove your worth. It may just be my own perception, but it means you cannot always speak your mind, and you always feel that you have to justify yourself – which is tiring.'

But Horvat brims with enthusiasm when speaking about her students at Queen Margaret University. 'I have taught many of the playwrights, dramaturgs and producers of the future. Many have established their own theatre companies which is a source of much pride for me. I put my own writing career as a playwright on hold to invest in the new generation.'

She reflects. 'Yes, I guess that's my contribution to Scotland. And Scotland may just have turned out to be the greatest love of my life.'

14

Why Not? Why Ever Not?

If you have no confidence in self, you are twice defeated in the race of life. With confidence, you have won even before you have started. –
Marcus Tullius Cicero

THE FINAL YEAR of my degree flew by. I read a lot, studied a lot and got to grips with running a household with my – had this really happened? – husband. We had no idea what we were doing, of course. We were 22 years of age, for goodness' sake! Nevertheless, the arrogance of youth prevailed once more. If you remain convinced that you can do something, lo and behold, it often turns out that you can. In some ways it was a sad year, with friends moving away and dispersing to the four corners of the earth. Chris would take the plunge and move to America, and ultimately marry the girlfriend he'd met during summer camps. Sharon applied for jobs in London. All around us, people were making big decisions.

I was preoccupied. I had always thought I might write one day. I expected that I would teach one day. But I hadn't, until that moment, thought through the consequences of this. If I was going to base myself in Scotland, could I hope to teach the subject I now had a Master's degree in? Would anyone employ an English teacher who was not even a native speaker?

I voiced these concerns, tentatively, to my lecturer Professor Giegerich during a final visit to his office, disguised in a semi-humorous remark: 'Ha ha, now the job hunt starts. I thought about teaching, but I'm not really English teacher material, am I?'

He wasn't smiling. He looked at me in genuine alarm.

I shrugged. 'Well, I can't very well teach English in a secondary school here, can I? They won't want a foreigner teaching their kids Shakespeare, will they?'

He stared, his forehead furrowing. There was little pause before he answered with total bafflement. 'Why not? Why ever not?'

I had no answer to that. Right in front of me was proof that somebody with an accent and a foreign passport could be Professor of English Language at one of the country's top universities – and I was worrying about secondary schools?

I often think back to that moment. It was pivotal in many ways. Could I teach here? Of course I could – I had exactly the same qualification as every other English teacher in the country, a degree in the subject. Later the question in my mind would be: can I write books in English? Will a publisher here touch a non-native writer with a bargepole? And I reminded myself of the baffled expression and the hint of outrage in the professor's voice. *Why not? Why ever not?*

As far as mantras go, this one's good enough for me. I'd choose this one as my modus operandi.

But perish the thought! My rushed application to teacher training college resulted in a rejection. It felt like a defeat of epic proportions. I was still unaccustomed to rejection, I had never even missed out on a job I had applied for, nor failed anything other than my first driving test. Maybe I wasn't meant to be a teacher after all?

Again, the little voice echoed in my mind. *Why not? Why ever not?*

I needed experience, that was all! Then, if I reapplied, I would have new things to say. Better things. I would be better informed. I spent some months running an after-school club for a primary school – it was a baptism of fire and is still one of the most challenging jobs I have ever done. Never before had I dealt with ADHD or autism, for example. I was in my early 20s and now in sole charge of meeting the needs of every child, from four to twelve – and wherever you looked, there seemed to be millions of them! On the upside, being an after-school-club leader gave me the mornings free, which opened the door for another form of education experience: I was hired to cover the librarian's lunch hour at a private school nearby. It was my first encounter with the independent school sector. It was simply unlike anything I had ever come across at home where independent schools rarely existed and home schooling was illegal. Walking from the bus stop at Murrayfield up to Ravelston, I marvelled at the leafy environment, so very different from the Old Town bustle I was used to and had come to equate with Edinburgh.

I tentatively introduced myself at reception and a smartly dressed, prim teacher who looked as if she had walked straight out of an Enid Blyton novel led me to the staffroom, pointing out beautiful buildings and astonishing resources left and right, and name-dropping famous alumni. Come to think of it, I had never set foot in an all-girls' establishment before, and schools in Germany had looked very different: no school uniform for a start. All of this seemed positively antique to me.

'So, you're taking a year out after university?' the Blytonesque Miss asked.

'Yes. I am trying to get some experience in schools before applying to teacher training.' I bit my tongue at the disgrace – 'reapplying' would have been more truthful.

'Well, let's see what we can do about that. English was your subject, you say?'

Before I knew what was happening, she had hustled over a colleague nearby, one from the school's English department. A week later I was sitting and observing her lessons – a masterclass in how to engage teenagers in literature. The week after that, I found myself in front of her class of 17-year-olds, leading my very first school discussions on Glasgow playwright Rona Munro's *Bold Girls*. I was 23. I had had many reservations about private education, and I still do. But without a doubt, the school's independence made it nimble; less constrained about what they could and couldn't do. I had no teaching qualification, and I wasn't even enrolled on a teaching course. And yet I was trusted with classes, supervised and encouraged, with detailed feedback on content and methodology, for several months. They had decided to help me, and no guideline or rule was going to stand in their way. It was a generous thing to do, and I will always be grateful for it.

I reapplied to Moray House College of Education and waited. In my interview, I gave less cringeworthy and more nuanced answers. And, finally the letter arrived – I was going to train as a teacher!

But if I was going to study full-time again, we would need to find some money from somewhere – my husband's student grant as a medic would not support us both, even with the additional allowance for me as a dependent. Now that my place on the course was secure, money was king.

With a heavy heart I quit both schools and began work as a receptionist in a small hotel on Grove Street, close to Haymarket Station. The pay wasn't exactly generous, but at least Edinburgh's busy tourist traffic would guarantee a steady supply of hours. Besides, I'd be in the office on my own most of the time. Best of all, I was allowed to read! Conveniently, the hotel was only a short walk away from our tiny rented Tollcross flat ('too small to swing a cat', according to our friends).

The irony wasn't lost on me – here I was, a German, wearing tartan, handing out Edinburgh maps and being the face of Scotland to guests from all over the world. A cheerful smile was all it took to succeed here – this was my kind of job! The clearest memory of that time, however, is of a more sombre moment. It was 13 March 1996. Listening to the office radio which was my constant companion when I wasn't reading, I heard that a man called Thomas Hamilton had walked into Dunblane Primary School near Stirling that day, shot 16 children and one teacher dead and injured 15 others, before killing himself. Scotland's darkness, it would appear, was not limited to its stories.

I wasn't a mother then, and I wasn't a teacher yet, but I was deeply troubled.

This was *my* Scotland, violated and hurting.

Lorenzo Conti – Italy

'Every time I think of leaving Scotland, something happens, and I end up staying,' laughs Lorenzo Conti. 'First my undergraduate at the University of Edinburgh, then my M.Eng., then my PhD, and now Crover, my start-up.'

That the young Italian scientist-turned-entrepreneur is Scotland's gain is beyond doubt. While researching his doctorate in granular physics at the University of Edinburgh, Lorenzo developed a robotic device which helps farmers and grain merchants monitor conditions in their silos and maintain grain quality. Less spoilage of these valuable crops is a crucial step towards food sustainability. 'It basically works like an underground drone, moving through solid grains and building up a 3D map of moisture and temperature,' he explains.

The company and its founder have already picked up a sizeable clutch of awards, including a Wild Card EDGE award at Scotland's largest entrepreneurial competition, a Shell LiveWIRE Smarter Future award and, perhaps most impressively, coming third in the Climate Launchpad Grand Final, the top global green business competition – the highest scoring Scottish team ever. Conti is pleased: 'I suppose I wanted to make an impact, make a contribution – and Crover has done that.'

He considers himself a mixture of Scotland and Italy after more than a decade in his adopted homeland here. 'There are so many memories, so many things I love about Edinburgh. I grew up in the centre of Rome, so you can say I swapped one UNESCO heritage site for another! One of my first meals was in the Witchery by the Castle. I thought, "Wow, Scottish food is good!" I love seafood and I even like haggis – some of my Italian friends are horrified by what I eat. And I like to crash random ceilidhs!'

He was visiting Cambridge for his brother's graduation during the week of the 2016 Brexit vote. 'Cambridge is such a thriving place. The morning of the result, however, the place looked like a ghost town. All that was missing was the tumbleweed. There was such a sadness. It felt like the death of intellect.'

Like many other Europeans in Scotland, he values what Scotland offers while appreciating the culture of his homeland, too. 'I basically take the best bits of both cultures,' he smiles. 'But so many high points of my life have been here in Scotland, my qualifications, my career, my relationships.'

What would he say to Scotland?

He is thoughtful, searching for the right expression.

'Ah, got it,' he finally says. 'I'd say go for it, Scotland. Gie it laldy!'

Sven Werner, artist, filmmaker and composer
(Photo: David Russon)

Professor Sir Anton Muscatelli, economist and Principal of the
University of Glasgow (University of Glasgow Photographic Unit)

WG Saraband, artist and political activist
(Photo: Roger Gonçalves)

Professor Daniela Sime, academic
(Photo: Jordi Sala-Ibañez)

Lorenzo Conti, scientist and entrepreneur (Photo: Matthew Hopper)

Daiva Ivanauskaitė, storyteller
(Photo: Gintarė Kulytė)

Tim Visser, rugby player, at his rugby club in Hilversum, Holland; his da
and uncle are shown in the team photo behind him
(Photo: Marcel Krijger)

Petra Wetzel, brewer and entrepreneur (Photo: Chris Steele Perkins/Magnum Photography)

Gio Benedetti, innovator, entrepreneur

Eddy Graham, academic
(Photo: June Graham)

Andreas Basekis, software engineer

Julija Pustovrh, designer and ceramicist (Photo: Matjaz Vidmar)

Krystyna Irena Szumelukova, town planner and campaigner

Martin Cingel, ice hockey player and coach (Photo: Karl Denham)

Ioannis Panayiotakis, volleyball coach and school librarian. Pictured (left) in his national coaching role for Volleyball Scotland

Peter Haring, professional footballer (Photo: David Mollison, reproduced courtesy of Heart of Midlothian FC)

Dr Andreas Herfurt, GP, guitar builder and biker

Right: Evija Laivina, visual artist and photographer

Tania Czajka, Early Years Education specialist and puppeteer
(Photo: Dan Tsitilis)

Lotte Glob, ceramicist and sculpturist
(Photo: Martina Macleod)

Ann Giles, 'The Bookwitch' blogger, pictured (left) at Edinburgh
International Book Festival, with her favourite author, Meg
Rosoff (Photo: Ian Giles)

Jana McNee, physiotherapist and Pilates instructor
(Photo: Gregor McNee)

Thomas Farrugia, geneticist and entrepreneur (Photo: Stephen Gilligan)

Christian Allard, politician (Photo: Stephanie Allard)

Kristian Tapaninaho, pizza oven entrepreneur
(Photo: Jukka Salminen)

Silviya Mihaylova, pianist (Photo: Olga Kaliszer)

Lina Langlee, literary agent
(Photo: Andrew Seagrave)

Maria de la Torre, environmental lawyer
(Photo: Murray Ferguson)

15

Teaching

It is a grand thing to rise in the world. The ambition to do so is the very salt of the earth. It is the parent of all enterprise, and the cause of all improvement. – Anthony Trollope

'ARE YOU SURE you're okay with this?' Rob stared in turn at the bulging suitcase and my distinctly watery eyes.

'Of course! Yeah! Definitely!'

Maybe I had protested a little too hard there, but I meant it. I wanted him to enjoy a proper medical elective, just as he would have done had he not been married. Reluctantly, he had made arrangements to spend a couple of months in Germany in a children's hospital not far from my parents – an opportunity to learn more of my language and understand my culture a little better – followed by three months in a hospital in Nazareth, a Palestinian town in Israel. I didn't want him to miss out on his adventure because of the ring on his finger. But there was no mistaking it, I was wobbling, and I hated myself for it.

They say that good things come to those who wait. I had waited for a year to begin teacher training and now I was about to start! Granted, my new husband was about to fly off into the big wide world, but I would wait for him to come back and appreciate him much more than before, I told myself. Get a grip, Barbara! I waved him off and sobbed my way back to the airport bus to return to our empty flat in Tollcross. Just me and the mice then, apart from good friends like Rob's thoughtful pal Martin who checked on me often. Rob must have asked him to.

At least I had something to get my teeth into. I was determined to make a success of my teacher training year. University had been full of distractions, a much too active social life, and endless excuses to cut corners. I had missed out on my predicted 2:1 by a single per cent. This year I'd turn over a new leaf. I would not just pass, I vowed. No, I would excel!

Making new friends was easy. On my first day, I met lovely Elaine from Dumfries. I particularly took to an English girl called Rachel who remains a very good friend. It was soon evident that she had also vowed to do well and a good-natured rivalry between us emerged. The three of us would stride up and down the Royal Mile and inhabit the corridors of Moray House, bridging the gaps between lectures with coffee and conversation. For the first time in my life, I completed every assignment early. At nights, I would sit at the tiny table in the flat and read over lecture notes to the subtle rustle of mice beneath our washing machine. My mother had sent me a humane mousetrap in the post from Germany, but the pests rarely made an appearance, preferring instead to unsettle me with their noise alone. But that night, something caught my eye – a tiny, fluffy ball rolled out from under the washing machine. Had these mice had babies beneath my laundry? I was revolted and fascinated in equal measure, but I couldn't stop staring, frozen as I was. The mouse inched towards the mousetrap. Could it smell the cheese in it? I held my breath. Slowly and searchingly, it crawled into the tiny cage of the trap. I waited.

The miniscule mouse made itself comfortable by the cheese and munched. *Why wasn't the trap closing?* I had to take things into my own hands. Carefully, I reached across the table for my pencil case. In a lightning fast movement, I took aim and hurled it at the mousetrap. The fluffball shot out of the tiny cage and disappeared beneath the washing machine once more. About five seconds later, and in slow motion, the door of the trap creaked shut.

The next day the trap went in the bin and I moved the washing machine out to block every gap with broken glass and scrunched-up plastic bags. Enough was enough!

Thankfully I was having more success with my course. I loved it! Training to teach both English and Modern Languages was certainly challenging, but I found that with a little work, most of the tasks came easily to me. My first placement was in Craigroyston in Edinburgh's Muirhouse area which proved challenging to say the least. The S4 class I was assigned to alternated between impossibly lively and comatose.

One girl in particular barely lifted her head off the desk for the whole German lesson.

'What do I do about that?' I asked my mentor, desperate for strategies. 'Leave her for now and be gentle,' she advised. You can only make so much progress in a generation. Her parents weren't even in school at this age. She's here. That's progress.'

I wasn't sure how I felt about that. It seemed defeatist to me, but there was a pragmatism which I needed to take on board too. I was meeting a different kind of Scotland from the one I had encountered so far. A Scotland of substance abuse and teenage pregnancy and hopelessness, but also a Scotland of incredible resilience. I will never forget the 16-year-old girl who didn't miss a day of her Higher English class, pushing the buggy with her baby into the school with her head held high. The school operated a nursery for her and others in her position. I was full to bursting with admiration for her ambition! Her dissertation was on Irvine Welsh's *Trainspotting* which was new and edgy then, popularised by the recent film. *Was this appropriate for school kids?* Ach, what did I know – it connected with her and that was all that mattered. Wimp that I am, I skipped the more graphic passages in my preparation – I was not made of such stern stuff as the Muirhouse youth, clearly.

My second placement, not long after, took me to the leafy grounds of George Watson's College, a throwback to the private school world I had encountered in my year out. Fourteen-year-olds were reading whole Shakespeare plays, second years were analysing Yeats. I couldn't help but be impressed, especially considering where I had just come from. I loved that placement too, in the way that you do when something is not quite the real world. My supervisors and colleagues in both placements were wonderful and supportive and I gained in confidence daily.

By the time Rob returned from his travels, I was almost ready to graduate. My final report and the results breakdown pleased me greatly: ten A grades and just one B. Top of the class, surely!

My dear friend Rachel had been peeking over my shoulder, her own piece of paper in her hand.

She got 11 A grades, dammit. Of course she did.

Andreas Basekis – Greece

Like many Europeans, talented software engineer Andreas Basekis came to Scotland following the major economic crisis in his home country, Greece. After graduating from the Technological Educational Institute of Athens in 2012, he worked in IT support in Greece before planning to move abroad in 2014. 'I considered moving to the UK, or perhaps a Scandinavian city. In the end I chose Edinburgh because of my English language skills, the software engineering opportunities and the work/life balance I'd heard so much about. An acquaintance living in Edinburgh highly recommended the city to me.'

Within two months he had secured a position as a software engineer in an education setting before moving on to the energy, IT, banking and finance sectors. Andreas cites the fact that there are 'so many tech companies in Edinburgh' as a major factor in attracting him to Scotland. 'I was looking for a city that is either a capital or big enough to give me good work opportunities, but with nice countryside as I love travelling.'

While he is not a local, he also doesn't consider himself entirely foreign either. 'The cultures of the two countries are completely different, but that can be good: I have brought a different mindset to my job and I enjoy working with people from different cultures. I love how my career evolved from being unemployed in Greece to working with major market players for the last six years, doing the job I wanted.'

He has travelled a lot around Scotland. As a winter sports enthusiast, he recalls visiting a Scottish ski resort for the first time. 'I had to wait for a while. There is not really a snow season here – it's quite random. Anyway, I had a good time but when I was about to leave, I realised I had lost my car key on the slopes! I ended up speaking on the phone for hours with the insurance company trying to get someone to rescue us!'

When asked about Brexit, Andreas admits being taken aback: 'I was quite shocked with the referendum result to be honest. For months it made me feel quite insecure. I believed that there might be a time in the future where we are asked (or pushed) to leave the country. Thankfully, we are now past that. It didn't affect us much in the end, but I feel for future newcomers. I am still sad to see that part of the population feels that way about foreign people. Racism and xenophobia are major issues in many countries and that is quite alarming.'

But Andreas is settled here. 'Scotland is a beautiful country with a fascinating history and a bright future – even if I sometimes miss the southern European weather. Scotland shines in other ways. The very year we came to Scotland, we got our first pet: our cat. I think that was the moment when our parents realised that we were here to stay.'

16

A Foot in the Door

The beginning is the most important part of the work. – Plato

'I'LL GET HER a job. I'll definitely get her a job.'

Apparently, these had been my teacher training lecturer's words to the Principal Teacher of the English Department at Woodmill High School in Dunfermline in the early summer of 1997. I, on the other hand, was ignorant of her confidence in me and could hardly believe I had been given an interview at all. The old doubt had crept back in – who was going to employ a native German as an English teacher? All the *why ever not*s were clanging around in my cluttered mind as I sat on the train. Granted, it was only a temporary post, but the advert had stated that it was likely to become permanent. It was ideal, a short commute from the capital and based in Fife where Rob would spend part of his Junior House Officer training. We had even been offered hospital accommodation there. I really, really wanted this job.

For days, I agonised over what to wear. Eventually, I decided to splash out on a two-piece suit. Staring at the distinguished-looking lady reflected in the train window against the darkening sky, I realised that this was the most adult I had ever looked. I was wearing lipstick, for crying out loud. Who was I trying to kid? It was just me.

I've never been great with directions. It took me a minute or two to work out which way to turn from the station, but soon the school was visible on the horizon. Regrettably, so were the rainclouds. It is hard to put into words how forceful and unwelcome the deluge was. Before long, water was squelching out of my carefully polished heels. My oh-so-fancy suit stuck blotchily to my skin. I resolved not to even think about my mascara. To add insult to injury, a quick glance at my watch confirmed that I was early – very early. Still the rain came lashing down. What to do – step into the school and wait there, shivering and awkward? Or keep moving and getting an idea of the school's catchment area? I settled on the latter and picked my way up to Abbeyview, where I was taken aback by an assortment of broken windows. Young children played in the street, their adults standing some way off and smoking. I smiled in greeting but was stared up and down with thinly veiled suspicion. Few cars, open doors and a thunderous sky are my visual memories. I retraced my steps downhill, back to the school, and a particularly vicious downpour swept me along and through the glass double door. I clutched my sodden document wallet with my degree certificates. What now?

I decided to laugh it off.

'Good afternoon. My name is Barbara Henderson.'

The name still sounded strange. I had shed my obvious German-ness – Barbara Henderson sounded positively Scottish! The receptionist suppressed a smirk.

'I got caught in a bit of a shower, sorry. I'm here for an interview for the English teacher's post.' Before the receptionist could say anything, a small stout man in blue work trousers and carrying an enormous bundle of keys walked past. 'Dinna worry hen, I'll take it frae here.' He motioned for me to follow. I breathed a sigh of relief. I'd always got on well with janitors. I wasn't as nervous around them, and this one seemed quite a character.

'Is this the Rector's room?' I asked when he showed me into an untidy office with a single chair perched in front of a paper-laden desk.

'Yeah, hen, he'll be here in a minute.' The janitor strode to the other side of the desk and sank into the Rector's chair, clearly enjoying the shock on my face. 'He won't mind, dinnae worry,' he laughed. 'So, got a soaking eh?'

I couldn't help but laugh too. Just chatting felt good. I wailed to him of my mishaps, of the new suit, of being worried about being German. He'd worked here for ages, he told me, 'in wi' the bricks'. He asked me if I'd seen much of the area. I spoke of my walk, of my placement in Muirhouse, an area with plenty of social challenges too. At one point, he actually put his feet on the Rector's desk! I tensed – footsteps were approaching in the corridor. Dropping all informality, I straightened up, brushed down my crumpled jacket and assumed a facial expression which I hoped would ooze professionalism and competence.

The man walking through the door was a moustached middle-aged gentleman with an upright posture and a natural intensity. 'Barbara. Good to meet you. My name is Hugh Gallagher, Head of English. So, you've met the Rector then.'

My face fell.

'Oh, no, Mr Watson! Don't tell me you've pretended to be the jannie again!'

I was still speechless. 'Well,' Mr Gallagher grimaced apologetically. 'As you can see, Barbara, things here aren't always done in the conventional way.' He motioned at the Rector's feet, still resting on a pile of paperwork. The conman was wearing a self-satisfied grin. 'You catch folk with their guard down. See what they're really like. Now, Barbara, let me ask you a few more questions. In your application you say...'

I have little memory of the formal part of the interview, although I do remember walking past a queue of waiting candidates, mostly comprised of my fellow trainee teachers, on my way out. The clearest memory, however, is the phone call from Hugh Gallagher in the evening. 'Your interview was strong, your references were excellent, and we would like to offer you the post. Would you like to come and work with us?'

I'm glad to say I was not speechless then. I had been offered a job. My first bona fide job! Despite my passport and despite my drowned rat look, someone had seen fit to hire me. Me! We packed our bags and moved to Fife.

My first week at Woodmill was challenging and exciting in equal measure: the bottom fourth year set, the bottom third year set and the most challenging second year class in the school were all on my timetable. But I had also been timetabled for some Drama and soon I was given a lovely first year class and some Sixth Year Studies sessions. I felt like a proper professional!

In the staffroom I tried to smile at everyone. However, I was genuinely disconcerted when a wiry, bearded colleague appeared from the smokers' staff room and tapped me on the shoulder. 'Hey, new girl. Come for a drive with me.'

There wasn't a hint of friendliness in his face. He looked like a man on a mission.

Every alarm bell in my brain began to ring – this was a stranger. I couldn't get in the car with him. But he was insistent: 'Come. There is something I need to show you.'

I looked across the table for help, but my fellow English teachers only nodded their encouragement. 'He takes everyone for a drive when they start here. It's okay.' I took a deep breath and followed the man.

For the next 20 minutes, we wove through the back streets. He pointed at boarded up and broken windows, abandoned needles on the pavement, unkempt adults standing in the middle of the street with no urgency or motivation. 'See?' he said. 'Now listen! That's why we're here. These kids are going to drive you mad. They don't do their homework, they're at it, all the time. But this...' He motioned at the dilapidated buildings. 'This is the kind of shit they're going home to, so we need to hang in there. What we do is important.'

I will never forget that mission statement. It cushioned me through phases of self-doubt and frustration and pulled me back to the job day after day, even when it made me feel physically sick with fear.

In my three years at the school, many of the pupils did get into trouble. There were arrests for break-ins, a bomb hoax and countless vicious fights in the playground. I remember two pupils attacking each other with chairs in my classroom. I had to step between them, only afterwards remembering that I was eight months pregnant. I was told about one occasion predating my arrival, which had entered legend. A youngster was seen wielding a knife. Several members of staff wrestled the young man to the ground and the rotund Rector I had taken for a janitor simply sat on him. 'Get off me, yer fat bastard!' the pupil is reported to have cursed.

Not moving a muscle, the Rector admonished: 'Hey, hey, hey! Less of the *fat*!'

Hearts of Midlothian footballer Peter Haring hails from Eisenstadt in Austria and has become a firm fan favourite since his arrival at Tynecastle in June 2018. His first season saw Haring, initially touted as a defender, become an influential midfielder who went on to play for the club in a Scottish Cup final against Celtic in May 2019. 'You don't get to play in too many cup finals. That was a great experience.' He feels part of his community here now but also holds on to that sense lightly – after all, football is unpredictable, and it is hard to plan ahead. 'I'm here for a time, I know that,' he says as he prepares for a return to playing after a period of injury. 'I came to Scotland because the club asked me to come; I hadn't planned it. I remember being really nervous on the plane because I wasn't sure what to expect. On my first weekend, I walked along the Royal Mile – I can still see it! It was a sunny day, and you don't get many of those here. The city really impressed me!'

He did initially find it difficult to follow the conversation in the dressing room, and the quickfire humour in particular – the players' accents also took a while to get used to, but he took to the playing environment quickly. 'Football means such a lot to Scottish people, probably more than anywhere else I've been. People really care. They identify with the sport, and with the team they support. I love to make people happy by playing football because I understand how much it means to them.'

Travelling backwards and forwards between here and Austria, he talks about the difference in reporting on the Brexit negotiations. 'I was talking to my missus and we think that the whole issue was covered more in the Austrian media than it was here. People in Austria really cared about Britain staying in the EU. I was surprised that many Scots were ambivalent. She is hoping to move over here to join me, but that will be a bigger challenge now.'

He is reflective when asked about his relationship with Scotland.

'There are lots of great things about Scotland. People here care a lot about their culture and have a strong identity, a unity. But sometimes that can stand in the way of change. Be open to change. Change can be good.'

17

The School Minibus

Mishaps are like knives, that either serve us or cut us, as we grasp them by the blade or by the handle. – James Russell Lowell

'WHICH COLOUR ARE we going for then?' The real school janitor waved the paint chart up and down in front of my eyes, clearly exasperated with my indecision. 'I'll go with the blue then,' I sighed at last. I was still astonished that anyone would ask a 24-year-old newly qualified teacher what colour she wanted on her classroom walls. But the number of pupils at the school had dropped a little and every teacher had a classroom of their own. Isobel along the corridor had gone for fairly neutral colours. At the other end of the drastic-statement spectrum, Dee had decided that her Drama studio was going to be purple – I wasn't as bold as that.

'Sure?' the janitor asked, snatching the chart away and walking towards the door.

'Yes.' My voice wavered only a little.

'And the woodwork? White?' He was out of sight by then, his steps echoing down the long corridor leading past the English classrooms.

'Yes, fine!' I called after him, packing my schoolbag for the last time before the holidays. Six weeks off! And boy, did I need them after my ten-month initiation. I was positively giddy waving my most challenging classes goodbye for the last time. I had survived.

On my return the following August, I began to customise my crisp and clean classroom with unbridled enthusiasm. Beside the door, I created a display called 'Word of the Week' where I planned to display commonly misspelled words. I had unearthed a framed portrait of Shakespeare in a Leith charity shop – perfect! Posters of inspirational quotes hung side by side with visual reminders of literary techniques. I had even bought a houseplant for the windowsill. I couldn't wait to see my pupils' reactions as they walked in. I feigned nonchalance and pretended to update my diary as the first class filed in. I waited for the collective intake of breath and the exclamations of *wow*.

'Miss, really? Controversial!' was the first comment. I looked up in surprise. Others were shaking their heads in disbelief, pointing at my gleaming blue and white walls. 'What were you thinking? No' everyone's gonnae like that!'

One of my pupils from the year before was at the end of the queue: 'Oh, way to go, Mrs Henderson!' With glee, he reached into his bag and placed a Rangers pencil case on the desk. And that's when it struck me. 'Rangers colours, right Miss? Didnae realise; ye kept that one quiet.'

I shook my head. 'I just liked the colour,' I protested weakly, to uproarious laughter from the class and a scowl from the boy with the pencil case. 'Seriously, everyone, I had no idea!'

'Well, Mrs McLaughlin next door's gone for Celtic colours. She's frae Glasgow. She meant it though.'

Ironically, this moment – humbling as it was – formed one of the breakthroughs of my teaching career. Everyone in the boy-heavy class had been paying attention to my mishap and from that day on, I made it my business to follow football so that I could drop knowledgeable nuggets into conversation. To my astonishment, the technique worked. I began to have more rapport with the football-mad Fifers.

However, I was also battling a different kind of mischief. Picture the scene: I might display a commonly misspelled word like 'definitely' on my Word of the Week board. I'd arrive the next morning to find that the board now said something like *'Bollocks'*, equally neatly written on coloured card, and I'd hurriedly have to wrestle it down before Hugh Gallagher, my head of department, walked in to check on everyone.

Who could be behind it?

The culprit became all too obvious when I whined about this mystery in the staffroom. To my outrage, my colleagues were merely amused and diverted – but my mischievous fellow English teacher Gail was positively crying with laughter. 'It was you!' I managed weakly.

I should have known all along.

Teachers in those days were a different breed: radical, edgy and straight-talking to a point I found a little terrifying. But I often look back on those days with nostalgia, too. Schools were actively seeking out characters, not conformists. Are conformists as likely to inspire? I wonder.

We had moved back to Edinburgh and commuting to Fife presented another challenge too. Having obtained my driving licence in Germany almost a decade earlier, I now needed to actually get behind the wheel. Gulp. As so often, it fell to our good friend Martin to come to the rescue. He had a car and almost saint-like patience, which was a good starting point. He had put me on his insurance and we met in a deserted street in an Edinburgh industrial estate on a Sunday afternoon. 'Hop in,' he invited, and I hesitantly slid into the driver's seat while Rob clambered into the back. Gosh, I had never steered a car on this side before. Changing gears with my left hand? It seemed impossible! 'How do I get the engine on again?' I asked almost inaudibly, earning me a sharp sideways look. 'You turn the key, Barbara,' he answered pointedly in a mix of exasperation and genuine alarm.

The engine howled in protest. I drove to the end of the road at snail speed, stalling twice. The three of us of agreed without hesitation that it might be wise to take a couple of proper driving lessons as a refresher. That done, the cheerily chilled-out instructor lady grinned. 'You wouldn't pass a test, Barbara, that's for certain. But you're safe enough to drive. No less safe than the rest of us anyway!'

We spent £350 on an ancient Ford Escort. Another step to adulthood.

Back at school, and now commuting regularly, I was keen to organise a trip for my tricky third year class. As a group, they were amiable enough, but a comedy duo called Graeme and Chuck were constantly looking to disrupt my lessons – they hated English. Maybe films would do it? There was a free film festival across Scotland, with new releases at number of venues. 'We could get to East Kilbride from here, right?' I mused one lunchtime in the staffroom, looking at a tattered map of Scotland borrowed from the Geography department. 'Someone could drive the minibus.'

It turned out that the only person who was likely to be released from teaching that day was me. Once more, these are changed days. Then, it was perfectly acceptable for a 24-year-old inexperienced driver to take a minibus full of unruly teenagers on the road – on her own. My only defence is that I didn't know any better. We set off, my heart pounding. My strategy for not getting lost was simply to follow the signs. Rudimentary notes lay on my lap – our department didn't yet have computers. The minibus was around double the size of any car I had ever driven before. My youngsters remained biddable enough for the time being, but that could change at a moment's notice. True to form, Chuck and Graeme were producing a steady stream of quality banter and I began to relax, chuckling my way to the Kincardine Bridge. However, an acute sense of humour failure (how very German!) set in when I reached East Kilbride. This town was the orienteering equivalent of a torture chamber! Roundabout after roundabout, I built up my biceps in battle after battle against the steering wheel. Eventually, I pulled in to ask a passer-by. 'Excuse me? I can't find the multiplex and our film starts in ten minutes and I must have gone wrong somewhere...' It came out so plaintively that the old man took pity on me.

The instructions came in something like 26 parts which my crowded brain could barely contain. I was drenched in sweat by the time we careered into the car park beside the multiplex. Would the minibus even fit under the barrier? I was past caring! I whipped the pupils across the car park and into the building – *no, you may NOT go to the toilet!* – and at last we sank into the soft seats of the cinema as the opening credits rolled. I had high hopes for this day: a decent film evaluation would generate a much-needed folio piece for my class. In my zeal I had even issued each pupil with a checklist of techniques to look out for in the movie. The film was accessible and entertaining enough, a lesser-known Steve Martin and Eddie Murphy comedy with plenty of angles for my pupils to explore. I breathed a little more easily. The only other audience members were well-behaved, posh kids in full uniform – I was lucky if mine wore jeans the right colour – apart from rebel Chuck who for some inexplicable reason appeared in a well ironed shirt and school tie each day.

With the film over, we strolled back into the car park. I took a look at my watch. 'Oh my word, is THAT the time?' In the Scottish winter, dusk falls early and we still had an hour's journey ahead of us. I might have mentioned it before, I simply can't be late; the mere threat of it has the power to banish all rational thought.

Thankfully, the minibus started first time and I zoomed towards the car park exit. In my mind I was already three roundabouts ahead when I heard the crunch. To say I had got my angle wrong was an understatement. I had somehow wedged the minibus side-on onto one of the pillars guarding the car park exit. I swore under my breath. Chuck and Graeme predictably began a running comedy commentary, but the waves of appreciative laughter from the others barely reached me as I staggered out of my seat to inspect the damage from the aisle. I could see daylight through the side of the vehicle! My stomach swilled with bile. It looked even more dramatic from the outside. To add insult to injury, a tooting concert had now begun behind me as our bus was blocking other cars from leaving.

There was no choice – not really. I got back behind the wheel and slammed my foot down on the accelerator, tearing our bus loose from the stone pillar and pulling onto the road. 'Whooooaah!' came the collective chorus behind me, but I was deaf to both giggles and taunts. Before long they were too cold to ridicule me anyway – I had effectively torn a huge gash into the vehicle and the wind and sleet were sweeping in like divine justice. Intermittent shrieks from my pupils were more in keeping with my mood anyway. In my mind I was already begging in the gutter, having been sacked for damaging council property and putting pupils at risk. I was visibly shaking when I confessed all to the new Rector – goodness knows what he would think of me now. It wasn't exactly the competent first impression I had hoped to make.

To my surprise, he guffawed for some time before sending me to the janitor to sign a form. There. All done. I could not believe it!

I was shocked to discover that none of my students remembered a single thing about the film they were supposed to analyse for their folio. After all of that!

Time for pragmatism. To this day, there will be adults from Dunfermline who owe their Standard Grade English to a humorous essay titled 'When Miss Crashed the Minibus'. Chuck and Graeme went one better – they made up a song about the whole sordid affair, with a rhyme scheme, a regular rhythm and several verses. This was sung with gusto whenever they walked towards me in the English corridor which, regrettably, had several pillars. Graeme would deliberately crash into them while belting out the lines, much to his fellow pupils' amusement. I hoped it would get less funny with time, but it never did.

Benno Schotz (1891–1984) – Estonia

The Estonian-born sculptor Benno Schotz's sculptures are everywhere in Glasgow. *The Stations of the Cross* in St Charles Parish Church in North Kelvinside, a bust of Keir Hardie at the People's Palace, the Joseph Black Memorial at the University of Glasgow. His works can be found on a former bank in Sauchiehall Street, on the Mercat Building, in the Maxton Remembrance Garden. Perhaps most subtly, *The Psalmist* (1974) is located in a low-key location by the river not far from a former putting green. It's easily missed, surrounded by more noticeable public art located between the university and the Western Infirmary. It seems little more than a branch snapped off one of the nearby trees, but consists of gnarled green metal, with transitions between head, body limbs and staff blurred in its beauty.

Born in Estonia, Benno Schotz arrived in Glasgow in 1913. He had visited his brother Jeannot there. His family believed that Benno was simply checking on the son they had not seen for years, but Jeannot enrolled his young brother to study engineering at Glasgow Royal Technical College. Benno was in Scotland to stay. Both brothers became well-known members of the Bohemian Chess Club: 'Naturally [my brother] introduced me to his chess club, where my speech did not matter, only the quality of my play.' After passing his final Engineering exams, Benno Schotz took up work at John Brown's Shipyard, in the Mechanical Drawing office. However, Benno also took evening classes in modelling at Glasgow High School, and later studied sculpture at Glasgow School of Art. He became a professional sculptor in 1923. After his first solo exhibition in 1926, Schotz became Scotland's leading portrait sculptor. Highly sensitive to the individuality of his subjects, Schotz developed a reputation for working very quickly and preferring his sitters to move and speak to him instead of being silent and still. 'I rarely prepare in advance, because I always want my sitter to see what is happening, it makes for a livelier subject.' He became a naturalised British citizen in 1930.

In 1938, he took up the post of Head of the Sculpture and Ceramic Departments at Glasgow School of Art. There, he would influence the next generation of Scottish artists, including Hannah Frank, Stewart Bowman Johnson, and Inge King (née Neufeld).

The accolades are many: President of the Society of Painters and Sculptors (1920), elected a full member of the Royal Scottish Academy (1937), Sculptor in Ordinary for Scotland (1963). His art continues to be represented in many major public and private collections, not only in Scotland but around the world.

Like his older sibling, Benno remained active in chess for some time before finally making his choice: 'Let me warn artists against taking up chess. It is a thief of time. I must have wasted years of my life in the chess club... I had to give it up, for I had no more time for it. I had taken stock of my priorities.'

Had he chosen differently, Scotland's and especially Glasgow's public spaces would be poorer for it.

18

Home and Heart

I planned the match from that hour; and when such success has blessed me in this instance, dear papa, you cannot think that I shall leave off matchmaking. – Jane Austen

OUR TINY, RENTED flat in Glen Street near Edinburgh's Tollcross had served us well for the early years of our marriage, but after our stint in Fife, a stopgap in Polwarth fitted the bill. From there, we would look for a place to buy. I think I have now lived at 13 addresses since arriving in Scotland.

'We should have a flat-warming party!' I suggested. 'It'll be nice to have everyone round, and it might feel less temporary then.' A couple of weeks later, friends and colleagues from both Edinburgh and Fife filed up the stone steps and into our new rented home. This flat was clean and minimalist. I definitely didn't miss the small-pattern pink flowery wallpaper I had so carefully covered with a giant collage of Lyceum posters in Tollcross. Teachers mingled with medics, Germans with Scots and Brazilians, and old friends with new neighbours. I remember it as a relaxed evening of music and laughter.

Several weeks later, Rob's fellow medic and close friend Martin was round. The two of them often caught up over a walk. Rob returned with a smile on his face. 'Martin says he really enjoyed the flat-warming party.'

'Oh, good,' I answered absent-mindedly.

'He also said it was a shame.'

I looked up sharply.

'A shame that you meet someone at a thing like that and then you never ever see them again. Take Rachel for example…'

'No way!'

Martin, the thoughtful, kind, quiet and unassuming trainee GP had taken a shine to my bubbly high-flying friend from teacher training? I had seen them laughing together that night, right enough...

When Rob saw the cupid-gleam in my eye, he tried to backtrack immediately. 'No, Barbara...' As far as he was concerned, anything that could possibly, theoretically, make anyone uncomfortable was to be avoided at all cost.

But surely, we couldn't just let it lie either. In the end we agreed on a Burns supper – we had hosted one every year anyway. If we asked Martin to do the address to the lassies and Rachel to do the address to the lads, it might work. And if not, well, there'd be a whole bunch of other people there to dilute any awkwardness. It was foolproof – or at least as foolproof as this was going to get.

Was it strange for a German to be hosting a Burns supper every year? In any case, my party-piece was a well-practised song rendition of 'Ye Jacobites by Name'. I felt able to hold my own in this strangest form of cultural expression. We stipulated that every guest had to contribute a poem or song of some kind and got started on cooking the haggis. I don't remember much of the evening now, other than a couple of fabulous addresses which really set the atmosphere on fire. Towards the end of the evening there was an awkward moment. Rachel looked at her watch and said: 'I suppose I'd better go.' It was my cue, even if she didn't know it.

'Hey, Martin – aren't you going that way? Could you give Rachel a lift?' I delivered my line with confidence. Martin, unaware of our agenda but hopefully grateful, stepped in quickly, even if his home lay in the opposite direction. 'Sure. No problem at all.'

The next morning, I got a phone call from Rachel. I could hear her grin down the phone and her voice exhibited the excited tremble of a woman with quality gossip to divulge. 'Barbara, I've got to tell you something! You will never, ever guess who asked me out yesterday!'

I smiled into my cup of coffee. 'Go on, tell me then, Rach!'

As I write this, they have been married for over 20 years and although they now live in Australia, we are still in touch.

By birth, Martin and Rob were Scottish, Rachel English and I German. But all of us were Scotland now.

* * *

A little spot of matchmaking may have been a welcome distraction, but there was no getting away from it – it was time to take the plunge and attempt to buy a flat. The German in me balked at this slightly – what was the hurry? And why would we need to climb the housing ladder anyway? After all, in my home country many people rent for their entire lives and it didn't seem to do them any harm. Our patient financial advisor explained once again about making an investment, paying into your own pocket, being able to take control of your finances and possibly sell on at a profit. It all sounded so reasonable when he put it like that! It was decided. Having found a suitable ethical mortgage provider, the carousel of weekends began!

Who had ever heard of such a thing? All of Edinburgh seemed to congregate in each other's houses on a Thursday night and a Sunday afternoon, the standard viewing times for properties for sale. We had narrowed the areas down to a couple and it made for a frantic time, sprinting from address to address and trying to squeeze in as many viewings as possible. Invariably, the places we liked would be gone by the time we had finally decided we were interested. 'We're just going to have to be brave,' sighed Rob after we had viewed a Leith property. We bid a little bit more than we had hoped to spend, a little more quickly than we were comfortable with. The anxious wait began.

Eventually, the phone rang and the two of us wrestled over the receiver before huddling close so that both of us could hear. It was the lawyer. 'Is that you, Rob? The seller got back to us just now. Turns out yours wasn't the highest bid.'

My shoulders sagged and my eyes began to prickle, however much I tried to resist. But the lawyer wasn't finished yet. 'But the sellers really liked you and they are willing to sell it to you anyway. There wasn't that much in it.'

Our eyes met in disbelief. Did that mean...

'And? Do you and Barbara still want to go ahead?'

Talk about a rhetorical question! Soon afterwards we were at the solicitor's office to sign our names on the dotted line. Married, check, employed, check, homeowners, check. I could barely believe it.

That flat was going to be our home. Ours. If I wanted a picture on the wall, I could hammer in a nail. If I wanted to put up shelves, there was no one to stop me. We were going to be in with the bricks.

Moving from a miniscule, furnished, one bedroom flat to an empty three bedroom one, however, presented its own challenges. We had committed every penny we had to the purchase of the property. There was simply no money to go around for anything else, be that tradesmen or furniture. Time to go back to the basics and beg our friends. It had worked for the wedding, hadn't it?

The staff newsletter at school was first: 'Lovely colleagues. We are moving into our first flat and have nothing to put in it. If you have any furniture kicking around that you want rid of, now is your time!' The next weekend, we borrowed a friend with his van and set off on our collection round. A discarded red three-piece suite came free, as did a rocking chair and a beautiful glass-fronted display unit with a cracked pane. For a small fistful of bank notes we bought a huge Ikea storage system and a Victorian writing desk with leather top. The van creaked back to our Edinburgh address, and we were officially in business. Soon we were on first name terms with the Leith Walk charity shop managers.

When the time came for our very first home-owner flat-warming party, Martin and Rachel attended as a couple.

Dr Andreas Herfurt – Germany

A rural GP near Thurso, Dr Herfurt uses a motorbike to get around and builds guitars. 'He's a character, that's for sure,' the practice receptionist informs me when I first make contact. Perhaps that is why *The Washington Post* picked him as the poster boy for a front-page story about disillusioned medics leaving the UK due to Brexit. He has been instrumental in shaping the GP service in the area and reforming out-of-hours care and is well known in medical and music circles. Doctor recruitment and retention can be notoriously difficult in the rural North Highlands. Dr Herfurt's more than two decades of service in 'Mackay Country' has provided much-needed stability for his Sutherland patients.

Originally from Mainz, he moved to Scotland for work at a time when German universities trained more medics than the country could employ. His English was good enough and he opted for Scotland: 'I think Germans and the Scots have more in common. And Highlanders treat you like you treat them.' He is sceptical about the UK government's approach to 'controlling' immigration: 'Why should I be better or more desirable than the lady from Poland who cleans the hospital? She is just as important! Without her, doctors like me can't do their job.'

Despite some initial post-Brexit misgivings, Herfurt does feel that he belongs, and has decided to stay put for now. He recounts a moving memory which sums up his relationship with his community. It was a consultation with an elderly patient with failing eyesight who had recently moved into the centre of the village from his remote home.

'So, do you enjoy being able to get around more safely now, instead of having to walk by the road?' Herfurt asked.

'Aye,' the old man answered. 'But there are so many foreigners in the village now.'

Herfurt, still with a slight German accent, answered: 'You've got to be careful who you talk to.' I can hear the smile in his voice over the phone line as he describes the moment: 'The old man actually laughed and said: "Ah boy, you are adopted here anyway."'

19

The Little Blue Line

All things are difficult before they are easy. – Thomas Fuller

I KNEW. EVEN before the little blue line appeared in the window of the pregnancy test, I knew. I'd been feeling odd, nauseous, not quite myself. I nodded to Rob. 'I'm pregnant.'

Somehow, this moment unleashed a whole lot of inexplicable compulsions – the compulsion to sand all the floors in our flat, say. Or the compulsion to paint scenes from Winnie the Pooh onto the wall. To knock all the tiles off the bathroom wall with a hammer so it could be redone (I did this mere days before the due date), to climb Arthur's Seat when our baby took her time to arrive.

Around the date of the pregnancy test, I also inexplicably felt the compulsion to schedule auditions for a school show. My Drama colleague at the school was on maternity leave. There was only me. I should do this. If I was ever to stage a school show at Woodmill, here was my chance.

I sourced scripts of Charles Dickens' *A Christmas Carol* from a contact in Edinburgh and set to work. Morning sickness? I had no time for that; I had a show to run! We got started in September and youngsters who had turned my hair grey during the morning's lessons became sweetness and light for the afternoon's auditions. Previous school shows had always centred on the seniors. I wanted to run a show for the S1–S3s, to give them a chance to shine. Planning the show for Christmas time ensured that I didn't tread on any toes by messing with the end of year routines. The Rector gave me his vote of confidence, so what more did I need?

'A lot of help' was the honest answer to that question. I was confident enough as a director, but thankfully colleagues from all departments stepped in to assist me with lights and costumes and all manner of other technical and logistical challenges I hadn't even thought about. A music teacher played the piano. So far, so excellent. But who to cast as Scrooge?

There were two gifted actors, but a high-flier in my third year class just edged it. Chris had a good work ethic, ambition, charisma and plenty of flair. He also had excellent retention, crucial for such a wordy script. But his quieter friend Neil had also shown a lot of promise. As a Drama teacher you don't only think about who would perform the part well. Being trusted with something important can be the making of a less confident kid. These were tough choices: who needed this opportunity the most? After a little agonising, I decided to play it safe and began to write out the cast list.

There was a knock on the door.

'Come in.'

My would-be-Scrooge himself stood at the door, grinning awkwardly. His friend and close runner-up hovered behind.

'Can't tell you anything yet, boys,' I said firmly. 'Cast list goes up outside the Drama studio tomorrow.'

'Miss, I wondered... can you postpone the show?'

I nearly knocked my coffee cup off my desk. 'Postpone it?' I spluttered. 'It's a Christmas play! When would you suggest? Easter?' I joked.

'No, it's just that the date isn't that good for me,' the boy mumbled.

A frown began to form on my forehead. 'Chris, you've known the show dates ever since you signed up! What are you doing that could be so important?' I glared at him.

'Coldplay are playing in Edinburgh, Miss.'

I was stunned. 'Some band is playing and you're pulling out of the school play?'

'Well, if you could change the date...'

'Have you any idea how long it took to get a date fixed with everything else that's going on in this place? Are you pulling out?'

He looked at his feet. 'I am.'

I wanted to shoot flames from my eyes, burn that Coldplay-worshipping smile right off his face. Instead, I crossed out his name beside Scrooge. ~~Chris~~ Neil.

On reflection, I began to write the whole list out again. No need to make it obvious I had changed my plans, was there? The last thing I wanted was to for questions to be asked, and for other stray pupils to opt for a gig over Fezziwig. I didn't want to give them any ideas.

It was the first full-scale show I had ever organised from scratch. Inconveniently, the steep learning curve in my skills coincided with the exponential expansion of my girth. I recall staggering home in the evenings and barely speaking a word before falling asleep on our red second-hand sofa in those days. Day after day, week after week, ropey rehearsals inspired little confidence in the finished product, but I was keen to raise as much money for the school as possible. I hadn't mentioned this to anyone, but there was every chance that this could be my Wood-mill swansong. I'd begin my maternity leave and soon after, Rob would have to apply for Registrar posts in Public Health Medicine, his choice of career after GP training. In those pre-Covid days, it was considered one of the more family friendly medical specialities.

The performance itself passed by in a blur. I remember standing at the back of the hall, saying every line with the characters under my breath and when Neil, the boy I had cast as Scrooge, delivered his first big speech, I knew instinctively that I could relax – I was in good hands. In my experience, young people will rise to a challenge, especially when there is little in the way of a safety net. The audience laughed in all the right places, the actors' voices were audible, my young, colourfully costumed cast remembered their dance moves and positioning and the final rendition of *We Wish You a Merry Christmas* rang out with gusto, amplified threefold by the audience. *This is why I'm a teacher*, I remember thinking. Not the exam results, although seeing young people succeed in formal assessments is obviously very satisfying. No, the thing which still gives me goosebumps is offering young people experiences which will stay with them for a lifetime, finding new talents and widening horizons. Discovering what they are good at and giving them a platform – especially in a place where extracurricular opportunities were thin on the ground at the time. My three years at the school had seen me make many foolish decisions. What was I thinking when handing Chuck and Graeme, the cheekiest pair of third years, an expensive film camera, for example? But here, at the back of the hall, with parents cheering and clapping and the newly discovered stars bowing in the limelight, I felt I had got something right. I often wonder what became of these youngsters. The smiley girl called Christine who played the Ghost of Christmas Present? The too-cool-for-school Scrooge who drove me insane by not learning his lines, only to prove he knew them all in the performance?

I served out my remaining weeks at the school with a heavy heart. Where at the beginning, I had felt only nausea at the thought of doing battle with the same classes again, now I was seeing people I cared about and valued – people I longed to see through school all the way. Instead, I was packing my boxes for departure. To have a baby. To be a mum. *Oh my word, was I ready for that?*

Late pregnancy is a strange limbo-land. You know that your life is going to change beyond all recognition – but until it does you don't fully understand what is coming your way. I was lucky to have lovely friends who were one step ahead of me with small children while others were about to have babies of their own. Rob and I attended antenatal classes and socialised with the other young first-time parents. In terms of preparation, there was little more than we could have done. The flat was ready. We owned every essential item on the kit list provided by the health visitor. I had particular ideals about the kind of parent I was planning to be – measured, consistent, cheerful, inspiring. Needless to say, my child would be completely bilingual, too. Well, pride comes before the fall.

The baby did not arrive on the due day, nor did she bother to show up the week after. My GP suggested spicy food and a climb up Arthur's Seat which we duly tried, but even that could not tempt this baby from her cosy hideout. Induction it was. The following day I set off for hospital, squeezing myself out of the door of our newly decorated flat. The next time I would enter through these doors, I'd be a mum. It was so strange to think of it like that.

A brief cocktail of drugs to set me on my way and the contractions started. Oh reader, I will spare you some of the darker moments of my 28 hours of labour in the Simpson's Memorial Pavilion. I was so relieved when Sandra, a lovely and kind young woman I knew from church, was assigned to me as my midwife. Here was someone I knew and was comfortable with. But I had not counted on the transformative power of pain. As the contractions got stronger and stronger, I'd inadvertently use language I wouldn't ordinarily use at all, but especially not in front of a church pal. Each time, I apologised profusely. Maybe a stranger would have been better after all...

Be that as it may, after more than a day, our girl made her big entrance to the world. I remember it so clearly – the relief, the wide-open eyes, Rob clutching his bleeding neck into which I had clawed my nails in pain – he still has the scars!

Most new parents worry about the physical side of looking after a baby: the feeding, the sleepless nights and the nappies. I can honestly say that I wasted little of my worry on those things, although I do not belittle those anxieties. But my prevalent thought was another, and it terrified me:

Here was a brand-new human. A Scot, a German, a person.

And she was all mine to mess up.

When visual artist and photographer Evija Laivina arrived in Scotland, she saw nothing of the journey up north, travelling the A9 during the pitch-black night. The next day she took a walk along the Inverness High Street and cried. 'It was so beautiful: the mountains, the folk music being played in the street. I come from a very flat, rural part of Latvia. I fell in love with the hills, and with this country.'

Leaving her homeland in 2009 was a wrench. The financial crash had left Latvia in crisis. Her husband commuted 100km to a job with terrible pay. 'We did come to Scotland for a better life. We already had family here, it was a country we knew. It's hard to be a new photographer in a country in crisis, and it's scary if you can't make money. When I arrived, I spoke no English. There were English lessons in my school in Latvia, but I was terrible at it. I remember telling my teacher there, "I will never need this!" When I arrived, I signed up for an English course through the University of the Highlands and Islands before moving on to my art degree.'

Evija credits Scotland with making her an artist. 'Where I grew up, I couldn't even dream about becoming an artist – it would have been very difficult to get an artist's education in my rural, remote home, a long way away from the Arts Academy in the capital Riga. But here in Scotland it was possible. I loved studying. Now I want to give something back, using my creativity as best as I can.'

Laivina's award-winning, thought-provoking style certainly sparks conversation. In her research-based projects, she portrays reality through the fine art prism, using symbols, imagery and often dark humour. Aesthetic surgery and the virtual world's obsession with perfection is a key concern of her work and has inspired photography, sculptures and paintings. 'I seek to highlight issues and spark debate about human rights and questions of conscience. I'm not so interested in being a pretty-picture-maker,' she laughs. 'I hope that, through my art, I am contributing something worthwhile to Scottish society.'

She feels less strongly about Brexit. 'The whole thing hasn't changed how I feel about this country. It hasn't changed my circumstances, so I'm less interested in that side of politics. My experience in the aftermath of the referendum was a lot of positivity, people saying "we don't want you to go away". Scottish people are very welcoming!'

At the same time, Evija retains a deep affection for the country of her birth and its culture. 'I lived in Latvia 30 years – how can you forget your home country? I still cry sometimes because I'd like to go back, but if I went to live in Latvia now, I'd miss Scotland just the same. I only speak Latvian to my children. Between them, they often chat in English and sometimes I feel like I'm failing a little bit because my youngest prefers English. Actually, when I'm being strict, I talk in English too – that way she gets the message!'

20

To the Highlands

To have another language is to possess a second soul. – Charlemagne

THE BABY, IT has to be said, was a bit of a diva. She wouldn't sleep unless physically lying on one of us. Nights and days merged. I was tired, Rob was in the last months of his GP training and often came home from his final placement utterly exhausted. She tolerated no blankets. Other than physically holding her, the only sure way of getting her to sleep was to place her in a snowsuit and plug her into a car seat – not exactly a long-term solution. However, there were compensations too. My adorable elderly neighbour from upstairs had knitted our new daughter a whole wardrobe of pastel cardigans. I hadn't come across people like the Binnies before – Edinburgh through and through. Every night her husband would come home and whistle or sing his way up the common stair. But for us, the winds of change were blowing again: Rob's first applications for Public Health training had gone out. Wales? Aberdeen? The Borders? Inverness? Where would we end up?

These were the days before mobile phones. He set off on the train to attend an interview for two north of Scotland posts while I stayed home with the little one and waited on tenterhooks. He finally rang home from a public phone box: 'They've offered me the Inverness job!' he said, still slightly shell-shocked. When he returned, we did a little research – the photographs on the tourist brochures looked very inviting. Moving north was going to be an adventure and would offer a little predictability for the next five years. 'I guess we're moving to the Highlands,' I told the baby in the highchair.

Boxes were packed. A decade worth of goodbyes wasn't easy, but I was confident that five years in the Highlands were worth it – as a medic,

Rob had been used to working on six-month contracts and placements. Here was a five-year trainee programme which would spit him out as a consultant at the end.

Surprisingly, the small Leith flat we had bought for little more than £50,000 sold for a healthy profit, affording us a detached bungalow with a garden and views in Inverness. What could be more adult than buying a lawnmower? Daily, I pushed my daughter's buggy up and down the hill to the local community hall, the shop or the school.

Meeting our new neighbours came with an added surprise. It went something like this.

'Hi I'm Barbara. We've just moved from Edinburgh.'

The woman smiled. 'Great to meet you, Barbara. What do you do?'

I motioned at my toddler. 'At home for now. I was an English teacher at a high school before.'

The woman's eyes narrowed. 'Oh, gosh, really? We are so understaffed at my school. Come and work for us!'

And this is how I landed a job, in my very first week in Inverness. I protested at first. 'Our daughter is still so young.'

'I'll find you a childminder,' she countered.

'I'm pregnant again,' I confessed.

'We'll take however long you can give us,' she answered, and it was a done deal.

I must admit, it felt good to be back in the classroom, even if I was only working part-time. I had not realised how much of my identity was somehow wound up in being a teacher. No toddler turns around and tells you that they really appreciate that nappy change or the pureed avocado. Teaching afforded me a little lifeline of recognition. I'm not proud of it, but the truth is I needed it.

Nevertheless, my focus was my home life, especially when daughter number two showed up. I had already attempted to fill our days with earth mother type of activities, but the arrival of our beautiful second child cemented an ambition in my mind – these kids were going to be bilingual. The only one who could make that happen was me. According to Scotland's National Centre for Languages, a bilingual upbringing can help a child maintain links with their family, culture and heritage, develop stronger academic skills in reading, writing and language learning and enhance cognitive skills such as attention span, problem solving, communication skills and task switching.

I needed no further convincing. Up went the German labelled colour charts. On went the German audio books and story tapes. We sang German songs at Christmas and listened to German nursery rhymes. But there was a snag – my husband didn't speak good German and my children's friends as they grew up spoke none at all. As the oldest began nursery, these concerns were vocalised by my children themselves. 'Not German again! You can speak English, Mama. Speak English!'

Dinner times became a farce, with me addressing the children in German, simultaneously translating for Rob. They invariably answered in English with me repeating what they had said in German to teach them my language. It was the sort of linguistic ping-pong that felt more like dodgeball – and all the responsibility to drive forward this much-resented policy was mine. I don't mind admitting that sometimes I was so tired that I simply spoke English for an easy life.

I needed help! Contacting the German Consulate in Edinburgh I queried: 'Are there any German support groups in Inverness? German toddler groups perhaps? A German Saturday school?'

None of those existed, I was told by the friendly assistant. 'Perhaps you would like to start your own?'

Time for action. I contacted my local library which was a common haunt for me and the children. 'Do you know of any other families speaking German in the area?'

They allowed me to advertise – and score! There was another German lady in my very village, with children only slightly older than mine. Together, we asked around some more, and each new family added a little stability to our group. I found one of the recruits during an afternoon in a soft-play centre where I couldn't help overhearing a young father addressing his kids in German. It took all my courage to walk over and introduce myself and invite them to our meetings, but he and his wife were among the most faithful attendees of our monthly get-togethers. These meetings did not only focus on language, although that was part of it. No, we crafted paper lanterns for the traditional German festival of St Martin and walked the dark streets with our creations, singing the traditional songs under our breath. The older our children were, the more prevalent embarrassed lip-synching became – with enthusiastic voices only from us parents, re-living our own childhoods.

During advent, we baked traditional German biscuits and listened to Weihnachtslieder. German Christmas, to this day, is the aspect of my birth country I miss most. There is a glare and a glitter to the Christmas atmosphere here. Germans prefer the glow and the glimmer. Subtle, quiet, reflective, peaceful – even as a child those were the qualities which appealed to me about the festive season. Both have their place, but I really wanted my children to experience what I had as a child. Out with commercialism, in with home-made presents – this was what we wanted. As soon as the children got older, we wouldn't have much opportunity to opt out. Even now, we don't let everyone loose on their presents at once. We do it the German way, one person and one present at a time, to be admired by all before moving onto the next. Unwrapping presents can take all evening, and I wouldn't want it any other way.

Even in the early years of the German Group, as we unimaginatively called it, there was a trend. The kids would gather for the food or the activity and say *danke* and *bitte*. But as soon as we let them loose to play, they reverted to the language of the school playground. 'Speak German!' I'd remind them from afar, only to be joyfully ignored.

I fared little better at home. We were a sociable household, living on a street corner where people passed, just as I had always wanted. Children from nearby houses gathered in our garden almost daily. The plus side was that I had well-socialised youngsters, but of course they spoke less and less German. Again and again I tried, but it soon became obvious that I was fighting a losing battle. *Vorsprung durch Technik?* I felt more of a forlorn failure each week. I don't even blame my daughters for resenting my language. You can't very well support homework which has been issued in English by giving German explanations.

It is one of my greatest regrets that, over the years, I caved in. There may be more than 53,000 households whose first language is not English in Scotland, but mine was no longer one of them. Perhaps I didn't really face up to it all until one pivotal moment in an airport departure lounge.

I happened to be travelling back to Germany for a family visit with my children. Beside me was another young mother, possibly a couple of years younger than me. She was clearly resident in Scotland and her visit had the same purpose as mine. We started chatting, as you do. She was one of these intense types: 'How long have you been here? That long, wow! And are the kids bilingual?'

I squirmed. 'Well, I started in good faith, but it's been difficult...' At that very moment, my oldest interrupted to point out a passing plane through the window. 'Yes, I see that; darling. What a big plane!'

I turned back to my conversation, but the woman's face was a mask of disgust. '*I* always speak *only* German with *my* children,' she announced smugly. 'I can't believe you're not doing the same. What an opportunity you're denying them! I would never ever speak English to my kids.'

I was dumbstruck. *What gave this woman the right to judge me? How dare she be so direct – so German – when this was my own affair, and my family's? How dare she?* However, If I'm honest, the reason her comments stung so much and the reason I remember the encounter almost verbatim is that she was right. I despised myself for letting go of the goal. I had given in, settled for less. I would now have children who grew up feeling predominantly Scottish and whose conversations with cousins, aunts and grandparents would always be stilted by an unnecessary barrier.

Over the years, I consoled myself with the thought that my children were kind and well-adjusted. We had raised happy, healthy, creative young people with a moral compass. They recognised opportunities, chose healthy lifestyles, approached other cultures with respect and curiosity, and I could not be prouder of them and what they have become.

Perhaps it was not failure, exactly. I only wish I had persevered.

If I claimed that I wouldn't change a thing, it wouldn't be true.

Ioannis Panayiotakis – Cyprus

Ioannis Panayiotakis recalls returning from Paphos to Glasgow. At passport control his documents were examined. 'So, you are from Cyprus and decided to live in Scotland?' the official asked.

'Yes,' he replied.

'Are you mad?' the man asked.

'Well you see, my wife is from Scotland–' the Cypriot began apologetically.

'Well, then you are definitely mad!' said the officer with a cheeky smile, and let him through.

School librarian Ioannis Panayiotakis is refreshingly upbeat, 'People feel better about themselves after talking to me,' he states simply. He has now lived in Scotland for 12 years. 'I still feel like a foreigner,' he argues. 'I don't look Scottish, nor do I have a good enough accent! I do admire people's politeness and professionalism as well as their grit, however I do feel sorry for them for their diet!'

Initially, Ioannis worked at the University of Stirling as a cataloguer while also coaching volleyball. He then joined the Scottish Volleyball Association as a coaching manager before moving to East Renfrewshire Council where he now works as a school librarian. He is candid in his observations of the Scottish people: 'If anything, I see the need for more compassion and more self-awareness. Scottish people are sometimes too hard on themselves and they have a natural inclination towards defeat. It was hard to get Scottish athletes to realise that they could be winners! And perhaps the Scots need to become more emotionally literate too – people are very reluctant to talk about their feelings here. They put on a brave face, even if it destroys them. As a Cypriot I talk without filters, I can be emotional, I overshare. We Cypriots value family, companionship and compassion.'

Working for Scottish Volleyball was a wonderful experience. He became the beach volleyball coach of the Scottish Women's Team and saw the side beat Bulgaria for the first time ever at Baden. He says: 'Coaching the Scottish Women and the Scottish Under-18 Men made me feel very grateful to the country that trusted me with such an important task. Believe me, training at Portobello and Troon Beach can be a magical experience – on a good day!'

Now he enjoys the interaction with young people as a school librarian: 'I feel I am learning from them. Being successful at job interviews and being treated fairly has been a boost – in my country, nepotism and corruption is the norm. Still, I did once get into a fight with two men who were racially abusing me. Brexit revealed that a lot more people than we expected were fed up with immigration and wanted to control it. Scotland could have done more to stop this.'

What would he say to Scotland? Ioannis quotes the Athenian general Thucydides: *'The secret of happiness is freedom, and the secret of freedom is courage.* Rather than obsess over negative stereotypes, wouldn't it be better to appreciate the wealth, power and proud history of this country – and yet understand that Scotland can be better?'

21

The Pesky Passport

Virtue, if a pauper, is stopped at all frontiers. – Herman Melville

ONE OF THE hassles of being a foreigner is renewing your documentation. I once left my driving licence on a plane. It seemed ironic that I had to book another plane to rectify the situation – flying to Germany and submitting to the ostentatiously bureaucratic system of queues, long forms, furrowed frowns and fees.

By the time I had lived in the Highlands for a few years, my passport renewal became an urgent task. 'You really need to get your skates on about that,' commented Rob over dinner. It is one of his favourite phrases, one I still hear with uncanny frequency – that probably says more about me than it does about him. But there was no arguing this time. He was right.

I don't normally mind driving. But a seven-hour round trip along the infamous A9, navigating to the German Consulate in central Edinburgh and facing down German bureaucracy was going to be a challenge, and all before the end of the primary school day. There was no other option. I primed a couple of friends to step in, should I prove elusive at the end of the day, and set off. The weather was bright at least. I had an appointment, and as the mother of young kids, I was on my own for the first time in a very long time. Giddy with independence, I played my favourite CDs on the car stereo, singing along loudly.

You'd think that after a decade in Edinburgh I'd be familiar with its streets, but to be honest, little of my time in Auld Reekie had involved driving. I had no satnav in those days, which meant glancing down at the city planner on my lap whenever a traffic light turned red. Miraculously, there was an empty parking space outside the rather grand building on

Eglinton Crescent. I breathed deeply, realising that I had been semi-holding my breath for the past hour.

A quick look at my watch and I strode up the stairs. 'In and out' was the phrase I had used to Rob. I needed to sign something or other in person, I had to have my previous passport scanned, and of course the German officials had to compare my new passport photograph with my face to verify that it was really me. None of these things I objected to particularly. However, I objected very strongly to what happened next.

'Oh.' The official's voice rang with disappointment as she leafed through my document wallet.

'What is it?' I was drumming my fingers on the edge of her desk without noticing, already planning my route from here back to the Forth Road Bridge.

'Your passport photographs – they're not eligible, I'm afraid.'

'What? WHAT? What do you mean?'

'Sorry, but these are British passport photographs.'

'I paid good money to have them taken,' I protested, but she launched into a speech about dimensions and angles and guidelines which my confused brain simply couldn't follow. I interrupted her: 'Are you telling me that I have made a seven-hour trip for nothing?'

She nodded.

I exploded. 'That's ridiculous. Why did nobody tell me this? Is there a photographer who does take the right kind of picture? For crying out loud! I thought it needed to have my face in it. These ones have my face in it. What's wrong with these?' I waved the clutch of rejected visages.

'Hmmm. There is something you could try, I suppose.' In fairness, the woman seemed sorry for my plight.

'What?' I snapped.

'There is an approved photographer for German passport pictures in Dalry Road. You could try there.'

The very next minute I was sprinting down Palmerston Place towards Haymarket Station. Clutching my wallet, I crossed the road and cut into Dalry Road. It is a long, long street, but eventually, the little shop appeared on my horizon and I sped up for the finish line. I crashed through the door before the alarmed photographer.

'Can you take a passport photo for a German passport?' I wheezed, staggering towards the chair.

'Sure. That'll cost you about...'

'I don't care. Just do it please. Thank you,' I added as an afterthought. 'I'm really, really pushed for time. I've got kids coming out of school in Inverness in four hours.'

I straightened up. You're not supposed to smile in passport photographs, but on this occasion I wasn't even tempted. Right here, a scowl was my natural habitat. I barely looked at the resulting photographs – bloodshot eyes peeked out from flame-flushed skin, with my hair in windswept disarray. I shoved them in the envelope, lobbed a banknote in the direction of the photographer and shot back out into the street. I have never been much of a runner, but worry lent me wings that day. German-style, I pushed my way past the waiting crowd and waved to catch the attention of the official who had dealt with my enquiry before.

'Oh good, you got it.' She stamped the documents with gusto and handed me the finished form with a flourish. To her credit, the corners of her mouth only curled up a little when she inspected the photograph.

A swift glance at my watch confirmed my worst fears. I was in trouble now. I stumbled onto the pavement and was stopped in my tracks.

My car was blocked in.

By a lorry.

Two men in high visibility council jackets were in the process of clamping my car!

'Excuse me, what are you doing! HEY! What do you think you are doing? Get away from my car!' I yelled. They turned in slow motion.

'That's my car. I'm sorry, I got held up and...'

'These spaces are for residents only,' one of them began. No doubt these were the lines they were delivering to parking offenders with devastating candour every day.

'No-no-no-no, please! I've got kids to pick up from school in Inverness. In three hours. Please, I'm begging you.'

One of them started scribbling in a notebook, the other reached for a fixed penalty notice. He handed it to me. '£60 fine,' he announced as if this was a great mercy and I bit my tongue. His pal had started loosening the clamps on my wheels at last. I didn't want to jeopardise my chances of escape. 'Thank you. Thank you very much,' I whimpered weakly, until they drove off. I zoomed out of the gap.

It is possible that I broke several speed records on my way up north.

By a sheer miracle I screeched into the school car park in time with the bell, early enough to receive my skipping brood.

'So,' asked Rob over dinner that night. 'How was your day?'

Tania Czajka – France

Tania Czajka is an Early Years Education specialist and puppeteer from France who lives and works in the centre of Edinburgh. She has never felt unwelcome in Scotland. On the contrary – she remembers the aftermath of the EU membership referendum in 2016:

'There was a spontaneous demo on the Royal Mile in Edinburgh. I live on the Royal Mile, so it was really emotional – all the placards saying, "You're welcome here" and "We want you to stay". I was just crying.'

Her own love affair with Scotland, however, started much earlier. 'I remember coming to Scotland for the first time with my best friend and we loved it so much that we didn't want to go back.' After the completion of her university degree, Czajka returned to Scotland and embarked on an SVQ in Childcare. Since then, she has worked with young children in nurseries and with adults with learning disabilities, before finding her passion: theatre – and puppetry in particular.

A regular contributor to the Scottish Puppetry network, Czajka is best known for creating *Lapin's World* – a bilingual puppet show which she has toured extensively in schools and at festivals, including the Edinburgh Fringe. A picture-book to accompany the performances followed.

'I love making things! I have my French language and I want to pass it on to young children through play.' She began the process by volunteering in a number of educational and theatre settings before securing funding for her first show, which she toured across the UK.

Now studying at the Royal Conservatoire of Scotland for a Master's degree in Education, Czajka is aiming to become a fully-fledged Teaching Artist, making language education for young Scottish children her primary aim.

'What do I bring to Scotland? Nothing special, just my creativity and my skills, my language and my culture. That's it, really,' she laughs.

22

Puppet Power

One of those extravagant reliefs from the realities of life. –
Charles Dickens, on puppetry

FIVE YEARS IN Inverness had come to an end. We had secretly hoped
for a consultant's job for Rob at the end of it, but there was simply no
vacancy – we were going to up sticks once more. We were used to it, but
five years had been the longest we had ever lived anywhere, and two of
our three children had been born here. At the very least we hoped that we
might end up somewhere nearby enough to visit. Our wish was granted:
Rob was offered his first consultant post in Aberdeen and we cobbled
together all the spare cash we had to purchase a house in Stonehaven.

Years later, our oldest would observe: 'Mum, when you live in Stonehaven, you're always a little bit on holiday.' I wholeheartedly concur.
Once more, we opted for a house on a corner where people would
naturally pass. It was diagonally opposite the primary school, which in
turn sat at the beginning of a stunning clifftop walk to Dunnottar Castle.
The harbour in particular became a favourite haunt, dominated by cliffs
graffitied with 'INDEPENDENCE NOW'.

Settling in is a breeze when you have young children. The town was
small, our new church was small; the geography lent itself to community.
But I will always remember Stonehaven as the place which had a profound
effect on my creativity. With the wee ones nearing school age, I began
to explore my own interests again. The house where we lived was ideal
– it had outbuildings. They may have been draughty and dank, but
with a little work I set up a puppet shed, first hanging my collection
of string puppets from wall hooks and then spending the best part of
a summer wielding a jigsaw to make a wooden puppet booth. I was

proud of the result. Now I could create Drama projects on my own, theatre in miniature! I had always loved puppetry. German children's entertainment had largely consisted of puppetry, filmed for television by the Augsburger Puppenkiste, or in the form of travelling shows. When I had had a horrible accident as a youngster, my sisters got me through weeks of recovery at home with their puppet shows. My first Pelham puppet was a Christmas present when I was nine, and I had treasured my Muffin the Mule ever since, displaying it proudly from the rafters and adding to my collection over the years.

I began to write material – short plays with stock characters like kings and knights and princesses, with the occasional dragon thrown in for good measure. I adapted folk tales and created festive plays. Soon I met a fellow German who had always loved puppetry too, and we began to perform together for larger occasions such as the Stonehaven Harbour Festival. I felt as if I had arrived!

'Wow, that's so cool,' a mother commented. You never really see puppetry, apart from Punch and Judy perhaps.' Having grown up on the continent, I hadn't come across the rather bloodthirsty British version of Punch. The German equivalent is a trickster and a cheat, but much more of a jester than a criminal. I concentrated on other material which appealed to me more. 'So trad. I've never seen anything like this before,' said another parent.

'It was quite common in Germany where I grew up,' I answered. Maybe having a foreign background was going to be a plus.

I contented myself with performing for friends, then friends of friends and eventually strangers. A Brownies Christmas party? A birthday party? A woodland festival? Of course I'd do it. I became a Jack of all trades – I crafted the scenery, wrote the material, performed. I simply wove my skills into the performance: fiddle intro, recorder playing, sewing and acting – it was a time of great artistic experimentation, with some triumphs and a good measure of terrible failures too.

One day I discovered a plastic bag of painted beads in a charity shop. Among them was a beautiful painted dragon head, and a couple of misshapen pieces of wood. It wasn't...

It couldn't be...

It had the absolutely distinctive style of the Pelham puppet – only without the strings. Most of my work had been with glove puppets, but marionettes had always been my first love. What if this was a complete Pelham Dragon? I bought the lot and sprinted home to google how to put it back together.

Not long after, answered my mobile. 'Is that Barbara Henderson of Puppet Power?' a caller asked. I still felt a bit of an imposter in my performer role.

'Erm, yes.'

'Your name was put forward as a children's entertainer. You probably know that the iconic open-air pool in Stonehaven has been closed for a period? Well, we're reopening in a large capacity and we'd like to book you for the children's entertainment on the day.' Of course, I agreed. The money was good, and most of my private bookings came from handing out business cards at bigger public events, so opportunities like this were always welcome.

'I think I'm going to do something extra-special and perform with marionettes. Leave it with me.'

I will never forget that day. First off, the echoey tiles were a problem, as was the noise disturbance from the passing crowd. Shrieking children having fun in the water didn't help the acoustics either. I set up in a side nook with my booth and the ladder behind it. Marionettes are tricky customers. They look amazing when operated well and I had written a new play called *Dragon Mountain* for the occasion. The Pelham Dragon was my pride and joy, and I had painstakingly sewn a backdrop of mountain scenery. I switched on the CD player and mythical music for the show began to play as children filed in and sat expectantly on the floor. As this was a solo effort, I had taken no chances, taping my printed script to the back of the booth and hanging my puppets and props from individual hooks: the magician, the boy, the dragon.

In keeping with the location, all went swimmingly until the climactic scene where a battle ensued between the evil wizard and the dragon. I'm still not exactly sure how it happened, but somehow the two warring figures became entangled. Shivering with anxiety-induced sweat, I had no choice but to invent an alternative ending on the spot; one in which the wizard and the dragon unexpectedly make friends and fly off into a faraway kingdom together. It was my narrowest escape and, strangely, one of my finest hours. I'm certain that some of the parents had noticed what had happened but their story-swept offspring were none the wiser.

Almost three years in, we felt at home in Stonehaven, although we also hankered after Inverness from time to time. Every Friday, the *British Medical Journal* would land on our mat. I don't know why, but on one particular Friday, I flicked through it. Around a minute later I was on the phone with Rob. 'You know how you always wanted to go back to Inverness? Well, they've just advertised a consultant's job there.'

'Yes, I saw.'

We discussed it after the children had gone to bed. My husband was always cautious. 'I'm not sure we should uproot the kids again,' Rob said. 'To be honest, I'd have to be 100 per cent certain that it was the right thing to do. I don't know, something really outrageous like… someone from the health board there would have to ring me and tell me to apply for the job over the phone or something.'

We prayed about it, which is what we do, and let it be. A few days later I bought the Saturday *Guardian*, our usual weekend treat. The 'Let's move to' section in the magazine read: 'Let's move to Inverness'.

I shook my head. *Nonsense.*

The application deadline came and went, and we breathed a little deeper. It was settled. No more dubiety. We were going to stay. That was fine.

Until Rob rang me from work. 'Barbara, you won't believe this. I've just had a phone call from the health board in Inverness. They have decided to re-advertise the job and they phoned me just now, to make me aware. They wondered if I was interested.'

Better known as 'The Bookwitch', Ann Giles is one of Scotland's best-known book bloggers, reviewing books and events in her inimitable, forthright style. She was also behind a series of book blogs for the *Guardian* newspaper – and the well-known author Meg Rosoff started it all. Ann recalls: 'I was sitting in her kitchen in London – possibly being a nuisance – and she suggested I should start a blog, so I did, mainly about books for young people. I read children's books as a child. I read children's books at university. When I had kids of my own, I read children's books with them and didn't stop when they grew up. In my time I have probably reviewed a disproportionate number of Scottish books, but I felt it was the right thing to do. Big authors are always going to get reviewed, but lesser-known Scottish writers may not.'

Originally from Sweden, Ann hid her identity behind the Bookwitch brand to start with, reminiscent of the artist Banksy. 'I tried to hide everything; where I came from, what I looked like… but it slowly slipped out over the years,' she laughs. Now she is a familiar face at book events around the country, especially Edinburgh International Book Festival where she feels at home.

Her story of Scotland mirrors the experience of other EU nationals here. She arrived on an Interrail trip as a teenager, later met her husband and decided to marry and settle, first in England and more recently in her husband's home, Scotland. 'Scotland is much more like Sweden,' she muses. 'People don't seem to feel or behave like they do in England, they are more collegiate here, less status-driven. I arrived just in time to vote in the independence referendum, though it didn't go my way.'

Being an EU citizen has not held her back here. If anything, she argues, it can be an advantage: 'I do feel a little bit foreign here, and I always will. But that is a good thing! People make allowances for you. It is okay to be a little bit odd if you're foreign.'

The Brexit referendum, however, was a game changer. 'I love Scotland. But with Brexit, there came the realisation that I might have to hide, to some extent. I have indefinite leave to remain, but if they were to throw me out of the country, I couldn't take my husband with me to Sweden.' The anxieties of Brexit are very real for many EU citizens like Ann who now face unprecedented practical challenges, compounded by the Covid pandemic. Travelling, visiting relatives and renewing passports are just some of the issues complicated beyond recognition. While Ann is unlikely to move back to Sweden, she retains an identity beyond her passport. 'I live in Scotland, but my Swedish heritage is very important to me. You don't just stop being Swedish. But maybe you have to be in this situation to understand it properly – home is both.'

23

Loss

The gem cannot be polished without friction, nor man perfected without trials. – Chinese proverb

OUR JOURNEY BACK to the Highlands was a charmed one. We sold our house with no fuss at the height of the economic crash with the housing market in freefall. It went to an interested acquaintance. Soon we found ourselves tracing the outer line of the Scottish mainland towards Inverness, with three children in the back and a hamster cage in tow. All of the little ones would soon attend school. Would I ever return to teaching, I pondered? It had been almost nine years of mothering and puppeteering – if I didn't go back now, I suspected that I never would. Supply work in Inverness quickly turned into a contract and it was as if I had never been away. Meanwhile, my father had become seriously ill in Germany and my visits home became more frequent.

It took me a while to put my finger on it, but I missed the puppeteering. More accurately, I missed *writing*. Looking through short stories I wrote when at university, I thought, *these aren't too bad.*

I attended a couple of courses, bought *The Writers' & Artists' Yearbook* and set to work with a New Year's Challenge – could I write a children's book before the year was out? In evenings and in snatched moments, I set to work. This was everything that the puppet-scripting had been, and more. It felt good doing this. In fact, I found that I loved writing!

Soon I spotted an article in the local press about a writing competition. A short story, set in Nairn, a seaside town just along the coast? I could try my hand at that, surely! Over a couple of nights, I put something together to enter. That would do. I slid the stapled pages into an envelope and forgot about it until I received an email. 'We would like you to attend the prizegiving ceremony for the Nairn Book and Arts Festival Writing Competition.' It specified a time and a place, and I remember knocking timidly on my Depute Rector's door. 'I've been invited to a prizegiving for this thing. Could someone cover my last lesson so I can go?'

The day after the ceremony, the same thoughtful man asked: 'So, Barbara? How did it go?'

'I won it.'

'You WON it?' His astonishment matched my own. 'Bloody hell! Well done!'

It was my first writing success. I'll never forget the towering pile of entered manuscripts, and mine right at the top with a simple biro scroll: *First place.*

Meanwhile, I had finished the novel and duly sent it off to agents and publishers, just as *The Writers' and Artists' Yearbook* had told me to.

But my father's illness had taken a serious turn. 'Barbara, I think you need to come to Germany,' my sister urged. 'Now! As soon as possible.'

It was the day before my birthday. I made a hurried phone call to work, booked a flight, and threw some clothes in a bag. I distinctly remember wondering whether I should pack something formal and black, just in case. Was I jinxing anything by even thinking this? In the end I settled for a compromise: black trousers made the cut, but the blouse did not. The earliest available flight left first thing in the morning from Aberdeen. My only option was to catch the last train there, spend the night in the airport and fly out, changing planes in Amsterdam. It was far from ideal, just like the whole situation.

That night felt like the longest of my life. I sat in a clammy plastic seat under the glaring strip lights of the airport hall. Periodically, cleaners passed me on ride-on floor polishers. I remember praying for my dad – if not for complete recovery then for an easy passing. Around midnight I was done sitting thinking, and even praying. I rummaged for my notebook. Another writing opportunity had caught my eye earlier in the year – a monologue competition. The monologues should be from the perspective of a biblical character, but that was all that had been specified. I began to write, without much of a plan, from the perspective of Peter's wife, in danger of losing her own mother. Could I believe in healing for my father? Or should I let him go? I poured all of my anxiety into that one piece of writing: grief and passion and love and loss. By morning I hadn't slept a wink, but I was happy with the piece. *Happy birthday, Barbara.*

Nothing ever goes smoothly when you really need it to, does it? My departure was late due to frost. On arrival at Amsterdam's Schiphol, the plane's doors were frozen shut and we were trapped for some time. All the while, the clock ticked for my connecting flight to Cologne. For those readers who are not familiar with Amsterdam's airport, it takes the form of a star. I had arrived at the far end of one arm – they are endless; really, they are! – and needed to make my way to the middle where there was going to be a further security check, before catching my connecting flight. I sprinted, literally sprinted all the way to security. The queues were huge.

'I need to catch a plane,' I protested weakly at a passing member of staff. She gestured at the hundreds of people ahead of me. 'They all do.'

I looked at my watch. The gate for my connecting flight would close in 13 minutes and I still had to get all the way to the other end of the airport. It was enough to tip me over the edge. Resolutely, I walked past all the queuing passengers, right up to the entrance.

'Listen, I have to catch the Cologne flight. I *have to* catch it. My father is dying...' And just like that, my eyes spilled over. By saying aloud what I feared most, I had relinquished control. I stood sobbing helplessly in front of an irate crowd of strangers, no doubt all of them with their own reasons for haste.

I'll say one thing for the Dutch staff, they ushered me forward and through security without question. There was no time for compassion, but they gave me a chance. Once through to the other side, it was up to me.

I ran like I had never run before, weaving through crowds and knocking into walls and corners, my suitcase under my arm; I couldn't wheel it nearly fast enough. Puffed up, red-faced and panting, I thundered into the empty gate where the airline staff were in the process of fixing a chain across the door.

'I'm here,' I yelled, shoving my passport under the scanner and edging through the narrow gap. The flight was half empty. The stewardess told me that 11 transfer passengers had been booked onto the same connection as me. I was the only one who made it. Sinking into my seat with endless relief, I felt an odd peace. Whatever happened next, I was on my way.

The plane touched down and my niece was waiting, immediately holding her phone to my ear. It fell to my sister to break the news.

My father had died while I was in the air.

'Well. That's the way it is, he went home on your birthday,' said my mum, hugging me tight. I maintain that she is the most stoical and brave lady I have ever met.

Now I was going to have to buy a black top.

The church ceremony was meaningful but solemn. Standing out in the cemetery in the December drizzle was even harder. I entered into the warmth of the well-lit church hall, emotionally wrung out like a mud-soaked rag. I suspect most of us felt a little like that. The German solution to this is coffee and cake. I think it is Germany's answer to the Scottish binge drinking culture. There is something akin to worship in a German's affection for this most iconic of institutions.

In the country of my birth, funerals generally end with an open mike – everyone who has anything to say about the person can get up and narrate. Soon the room was rocking with laughter at my dad's escapades as a young man, at his practical jokes and covert acts of kindness. It wasn't false in any way – most contributions began honestly by saying, 'Wolfgang wasn't always the easiest man to work with, but...' There was genuine warmth in the room. To my surprise, I found myself wanting to join in, to be part of the storytelling. Despite the fact that I had been sobbing all-too-publicly only an hour ago, there was peace here, and community. Both of my parents had lived here in this town all their lives. I was known and cared for because of who my parents were and who my grandparents had been before them.

It felt a little strange to say goodbye to a house with only one parent in it, and to turn my back all over again on this place and its people. Home? I couldn't even wrap my brain around that concept at the moment.

Back in Scotland I returned to work and the busy parent's schedule of swimming lessons, music tuition and basketball matches. Every day as I walked the dog, I did my crying with German efficiency before returning to the house, taking a deep breath and getting on with it.

A few weeks later, I learned that my Easter monologue had been chosen as one of the competition winners. It would be performed in Princes Street Gardens as part of an Easter promenade performance in front of hundreds of people.

Lotte Glob – Denmark

Danish ceramicist and sculpturist Lotte Glob arrived in Scotland in 1964. 'I came in the best way possible,' she muses, 'on a cattle boat from Dublin into the Clyde. The first class section was at the front, the cattle were in the middle and we sat in second class at the back. I saw the mountains, blue sky, cranes – and I was hooked on Scotland.'

She has worked in Sutherland for much of the last 50 years, most recently in her sculpture croft and studio on the shore of Loch Eriboll from where she retains an international outlook with study tours from Australia to Greenland. Her work is exhibited nationally and internationally, but she also opens her sculpture croft and studio to locals and tourists for workshops and grants free access to her land which is dotted with ceramic art and sculptures. Lotte was obsessed with ceramics at an early age and left school at 14 to become a potter's apprentice – a love affair with clay which has defined her life and choices.

She once applied for a British passport, filled in the lengthy form, organised witnesses and sent the £250 cheque. Weeks later, the Home Office returned her payment and insisted she took a spelling test with a local schoolteacher before anything could be processed. 'I got so mad with the system that I didn't do it; I refused,' she laughs.

Retaining a distinctive Danish accent to this day, Lotte is a vivid raconteur. She recalls living in Scotland with her then-partner. 'These were the days before the EU. The local police would come round every year, to renew my permission to stay. Eventually I got a letter from the Home Office, stating that I was allowed to stay in the UK as "David Illingworth's mistress". I still have the letter – I think I'm going to frame it!'

She doesn't think much of the current paperwork either: 'I am so cross about having to apply for settled status! I have been in Scotland 55 years. I pay a lot of tax and I have contributed much to the local community in Durness which I love and where I feel at home. My ceramics work has brought so many people to the area and I have looked after my land. I just think it is outrageous.' Lotte was ambivalent about Scottish independence before, but now she is strongly in favour, although she dislikes the noisy part of the nationalist movement, with their shouting, their rallies and flag-waving. 'It alienates and scares the incomers and doesn't do the cause any good.'

When a Danish television company visited her for a documentary, she was asked if she'd consider a return to the country of her birth. 'Never!' she replied emphatically.

'Oh no. What's wrong with Denmark?' the interviewer protested, a little offended.

Lotte answered thoughtfully. 'Maybe there is something wrong with *me*! When I came here, I was a young tree. Now I am an old tree with old, deep roots. You can't pull it up. It'll die.'

SCOTTISH BY INCLINATION

24

The Power of the Pen

You can't wait for inspiration. You have to go after it with a club. –
Jack London

INVERNESS STATION GLEAMED in the early morning sunshine of Easter Saturday. I was on my way to watch my words in performance in Edinburgh. Ten years of a place gets under your skin – I'd lived in the capital not only for a decade, but for the most formative decade of my life – university, marriage, the beginning of my working life and my first child. I jumped at every chance to return, and what better excuse than this one? Auld Reekie made an effort for me that day, and she sure scrubs up well. It was an unseasonably cold day, one where the bright sunshine is accompanied by the crisp crackle of frost in the air. The first thing I did once off the train was buy a woolly white hat from the craft fair at St John's on the corner of Princes Street and Lothian Road. Extravagance? Probably. Necessity? Definitely. A vegetarian lunch from the crypt café with friends set me up for the day. It was odd having left the kids behind – with three primary school children who liked to stack their weeks out with activities, I rarely ventured far. This was a treat, a break, and an injection of hope after a very long winter of grief. I wasn't here as a mother. I wasn't here to renew a passport, thank goodness! No. Being a writer was the reason I was there that day, and it felt good.

The director of the promenade performance had urged me to introduce myself, though understandably, she was busy. 'Great to meet you Barbara. We loved your monologue. It was such a moving piece. We all cried in rehearsal. I hope you enjoy the performance,' she said warmly before bustling away. The afternoon was organised with military precision as more and more audience members arrived. We were assigned a colour and a leader whom we followed around the different stations, each with its own monologue. Mine was being performed on a steep section of Princes Street Gardens, with a washing line draped between trees. It was utterly surreal to see the same words which had got me through my anxious night at Aberdeen Airport, spoken with such confidence here. We stood and listened, with the bustle of Princes Street in the distance, under a blue sky slashed with vapour trails of planes long gone. Again and again, I unfolded the programme to take another look at the list of writers. *Barbara Henderson.* My name was there, in black and white. Hundreds of people like me were milling from station to station and enjoying the performances.

'That was wonderful,' I mouthed to my friend, choked.

To this day, when I arrive back into Edinburgh Waverley Station on the train and look up towards the castle against the midday sun, I think of that moment – of the colourful spectacle of an Easter weekend, hundreds of audience members on the move and of my own journey from station to station: student, teacher, wife, mother, writer. Beyond the clouds, the sky is blue.

Memories of that day would become nourishment for the years to come.

What lay ahead were many moments of writer-doubt and countless near misses. I continued to set aside time to write whenever possible. Snatched moments in the dead of night, half hour slots before school pick up and ten minutes before bedtime.

Despite this, stories streamed onto the page. My first novel *Rain on the Roof* wasn't too badly written I thought. I submitted it to a handful of agents. Two of them asked to see more, which in itself was a holy grail. I was encouraged. Little did I know that another 120 rejections were going to lie ahead before I was going to have a book published – if I had known it, I might have given up there and then. One of my favourite stories to tell at dinner parties hails from that time. I had begun to research publishers in Scotland and had found a very small publishing company near Glasgow which had published a couple of comparable titles to *Rain on the Roof.* In a spontaneous moment of devil-may-care, I rang the number, expecting a secretary or an answerphone. The name of the person answering matched that of the managing director.

Flummoxed, I began. 'Erm, I've written a book that I think may be suitable for your list. Can you tell me a bit more about your submissions process…?'

I petered out.

'All right. Why don't you tell me a little bit about your book! What's it about?'

I am ashamed whenever I think of it. I now know what an opportunity this was, how rare. Unbelievably, I hadn't honed a pitch for *Rain on the Roof* at all. *Crap!*

I hesitated. 'Well, it's a pretty conventional portal story I guess…' Once I realised the idiocy of what I had just said, I slammed down the receiver. I physically *hung up* on a publisher who wanted to know about my book.

And what kind of book pitch was that? *A pretty conventional portal story* – who in their right mind would want to read that?

Upon a little reflection and much comfort-eating, I had to face up to facts: it was true. It *was* a conventional portal story, and no publisher would give it the time of day. Quite rightly. I needed a much stronger concept for a book. Luckily, the London Riots had sparked an idea which was already fermenting in my mind. Politics for 9 to 12-year-olds? Well, why not?

I set to work.

Little did I know that in the summer of 2013, my writing life was going to be changed beyond all recognition. Where? In a tent on the Durness shore in Sutherland.

* * *

Truthfully, we are not really an outdoorsy family, although we would love to be. Maybe this is why we fell for it: the too-good-to-miss deal on an enormous tent, 'all singing and all dancing', to use another of Rob's favourite phrases. It was an impulse buy and we coughed up the cash. A summer holiday under our own roof sounded like a good thing, did it not?

Having blown the holiday budget on the tent, we borrowed everything else from tougher, more adventurous friends and set off on the well-travelled road north. Family holidays had typically taken us to the north of Scotland or to the islands. The reason was simple – travelling to

Germany to see family swallowed up much of our disposable cash. What was left was usually enough for a staycation in a holiday cottage. This year, however, we were going to explore new shores. The campsite in Durness had an excellent reputation and Balnakeil Craft Village and its gorgeous café, Cocoa Mountain, beckoned. Durness it was.

'Why is nobody camping on that cliff-edge there?' I wondered aloud. The promontory jutted out above two golden beaches. Surely, it was the most glorious place to pitch a tent, was it not? The place would offer undisturbed views over crashing seas below and take us away from the hustle and bustle of the main site, especially the noisy clanging of the cooking hut.

We attempted to erect our tent, watched by a critical crowd of amused onlookers. It had looked much, much easier on the promotional video. Eventually, a seasoned camper rolled his eyes and took pity on us. 'Here, I'll help you. Looks like you're putting this pole in the wrong place...'

I brewed a cup of tea and left them to it.

This is the life, I thought as I allowed my eyes to roam over the clear blue sky, mirrored in the glossy water below.

Approximately eight hours later, I suffered an acute sense of humour failure. Appreciation for Scotland's landscape was thin on the ground. The sky had clouded over, and the sea had become a raging, spitting, frothing monster, ready to devour us. Our huge tent was battered by wave after wave of storm and rain. Being blown into the greedy waters seemed only a question of time. Invisible hands tore at every side of our flimsy abode and the children were beginning to whimper. I tried to lie down and ignore the threat of imminent doom, but it was hard when the tent floor beneath you lifts and flaps and shifts and the wind screams through every seam and zip. By morning – and I mean extremely early morning – we had to admit defeat. Dismantling our camp piece by piece, we weighted each component down with rocks. The children sat, huddled together for warmth, a little way off while Rob and I barely spoke to each other except in muttered curses. It took us most of the morning, but we had managed to rebuild our battered structure in the most sheltered part of the campsite, right beside the cooking tent.

As if to spite us, the sky had cleared to reveal glorious sunshine once again. 'Let's go for a wee drive,' Rob suggested. Not far from Durness we spotted a pristine, empty beach below the road. 'Stop the car,' was the universal cry. As if by providence, a small car park appeared around the next corner and we triumphantly pulled up.

Ceannabeinne Beach was everything we had hoped for in a holiday. The children discovered a cave and Rob was in the process of trying to get his phone torch on to light them in when I spotted some strange stones on the hillside.

'Hey, look at that up there. Do you mind if I investigate a little?' He shook his head. Our dog was tearing through the sand, sending a grainy dust cloud into the air behind him. I clambered up the hillside. There were unmistakeable ruins here. Before long I stumbled upon some signage: *The Ceannabeinne Clearance Trail*. In short, it stated that the landowner had evictions planned to make room for sheep. He sent the writ (the legal document compelling villagers to leave) on a day when he knew all the men would be away thatch cutting. According to the signs, the women and children of the village somehow managed to overwhelm the Sheriff Officer and forced him to burn his own writ before sending him packing. The event started a series of protests now known as the Durness Riots.

What a story, especially as touching the writ would have made it legally binding on the villagers. And it didn't stop there: when a more senior official came to deliver a new writ, the villagers were ready with stones, pelting the superintendent from afar. The situation escalated until the riots in the area were reported as far away as the *London Times*. I was utterly smitten with this story of courage and defiance, and astounded by the bravery of these villagers. How natural to cast a young girl as the heroine of the piece. Before I had finished walking the trail, I knew that this would become my next story. Years later, it would be published as *Fir for Luck*.

Something much more immediate occupied me on that holiday. In the sketchy internet reception of our tent, I had received an email. Incredibly, my manuscript had been shortlisted for the Kelpies Prize, a prestigious prize for new children's fiction set in Scotland. The winner would be published and receive £2,000. My gamble with politics in children's fiction had paid off. Plan A was back on track.

The Kelpies Prize ceremony took place at the Edinburgh International Book Festival a month or so later and my gregarious eight-year-old son was wowing the audience with his charm. I was all dressed up and ready to meet publishers, agents and writers I admired. For once, I was not on the outside looking in. As one of three shortlistees, I listened to an extract of my work being read aloud by the well-known children's author Janis Mackay. I enjoyed mingling with people whose faces I recognised from the back of book covers. In short, the evening was everything I had hoped it would be – bar one tiny fact.

I didn't win. My charismatic boy spent no more than a nanosecond commiserating with his mother before running off to pose with Alex McCall, the winner celebrating his giant cheque for £2,000 and his publication contract. As a runner-up, I went home empty handed and back to square one. The disappointment was real, but a day or two of licking my wounds were enough to galvanise me. No one had asked my nationality in this process. My writing had made it to the top of the pile, even in my second language. I was close.

To give up now would be madness. And I had just the story to pour my new-found determination into.

Christian Allard – France

A French-born Scottish politician, Allard is an Aberdeen city councillor representing the Torry and Ferryhill ward, which contains areas of significant deprivation. He has served both as a Member of the Scottish Parliament and then as a Member of the European Parliament until 31 January 2020, when the Brexit process was completed – all without ever holding a British passport.

His swearing in to the Scottish Parliament was conducted in both English and French, the first time that the latter language has been used for the purpose. 'For democracy to work, folk have to step up and consider becoming a candidate. In public meetings, I always say that if you are asking yourself why a Frenchman is standing for a Scottish election, you are asking yourself the wrong question. You should ask yourself why you are not in my place.'

An energetic and articulate man bursting with stories, Allard still retains a strong French accent. 'My English was terrible when I first came, but working with mainly men in Glasgow in the '80s, I only needed to know what the football scores were, and what had been on television the night before. It's not just the language – it's the culture! My experience has been very positive. Scottish people love to hear about people coming here from other countries. If anything, people listen to you *because* you have an accent, not despite it.'

A lifelong football fan, Allard felt his allegiance shift. When Scotland played France at Hampden Park in a World Cup qualification game in 1989, he refers to France's lacklustre performance during Scotland's 2–0 win: 'If a country of 65 million people can't beat a nation of five million, they don't deserve my support.' He switched at half-time and declared: 'We won'.

'What we need to realise is that the world has changed. Identity and nationalism are not what they were. People move, marry into other cultures, have children – my children are the greatest contribution I have made to Scottish life. The world is a village. And the right to vote should be extended to everyone who lives where the vote is held. I am no less Scottish than the Scots, and at the same time, I am no less French than the French. The two are complementary – we need to get away from this idea that identity is somehow static.'

Despite being a sitting parliamentarian at the time, Allard, like all other EU citizens, was denied a vote in the 2016 Brexit referendum. Was he upset about that?

'No, I was just campaigning all the harder, making my point in that way. I will always keep on campaigning. The day after Jo Cox was murdered – and that was a political murder – I took a T-shirt and a marker pen, wrote "I am an immigrant" on it and wore it in the city centre of Aberdeen to campaign for Remain in the final days leading up to the Brexit referendum. I'll always be an immigrant, but that doesn't mean that I don't belong. "It's not where we came from that's important, it's where we're going together."'[1]

---

1 Quote by Bashir Ahmed, the Scottish Parliament's first Muslim MSP

25

The Independence Referendum

The oldest, shortest words – 'yes' and 'no' – are those which require the most thought. – Pythagoras

SCOTLAND WAS CHANGING all around me. Huge wooden signs appeared in drives and fields: YES, they declared. I had been paying close attention – after all, this was going to be one of the few public decisions I was going to have a part in. As a European citizen resident in Scotland, I may not be eligible to vote in Westminster elections, but I was going to get a say in whether Scotland should become an independent country or not.

Noisy rallies passed by the river within earshot of our house and it appeared as if a disproportionate percentage of Scots had invested in a saltire flag. My social media feeds became political and polarised. Referenda are blunt tools: In, out; yes, no – it was counterintuitive, considering what we teach our children about the value of compromise. A referendum boils down to winners and losers, the Donald Trump language that does not sit comfortably with my collaborative psyche. And there was another layer – as I stated before, as a German I was profoundly uncomfortable with any kind of nationalism. Of course, Scotland's nationalism bears no resemblance to the 1940s Germany my parents experienced as children. Again, I heard the phrase 'Scottish by inclination'. In essence, what it meant to me was: 'You want to be part of us? Great, you're in.' I loved the inclusivity of the phrase. The simplicity of it. There was only a 'them and us' if I wanted there to be.

Still, I detected a bit of an unpleasant edge to political discussions – an element of guilt-tripping perhaps, and an unease among my friends who had come to Scotland from England. 'I just feel there is a bit of hostility there,' my friend announced over a coffee. And if she felt antagonism due to her accent, I am sure she was not the only one. Meanwhile, another English friend announced his enthusiastic support for independence with the clearest of English accents and joined the English Scots for YES campaign.

Feelings run high and I get it. Tearful interviews on television declared 2014 a once in a lifetime opportunity, the let-my-grandfather-see-an-independent-Scotland-before-he-dies sentiment. I was torn between arguments and persuasions. I had lived in Scotland almost all of my adult life and I felt that I belonged. Yes, I completely concurred that Scotland differed from England: culturally, historically, politically. But there was another powerful argument at play – 'If you want to guarantee staying in the European Union,' Theresa May, the then-Prime Minister argued, 'you need to remain in the United Kingdom.'

We were a household on the fence. I valued Europe over Scottish independence and my husband valued security above risk. In our hearts, however, Scotland deserved a shot at going its own way. So many policies made for the south were simply implemented without a mandate here and I had every sympathy with the independence cause. Nationalism which is inclusive and invites you in is attractive. Nationalism which defines itself by what it is not, less so. There was an undercurrent of aggression, particularly as the date got close.

It did feel like a big deal on the day. I walked down to the polling station with our dog, tied him up outside and took my place in the queue. Soon it was my turn, and despite the fact that I had thought about this moment many times before, my pen hovered for a while. Europe or Scotland?

Suffice to say that in the end, one of us jumped one way and one the other. In effect, the Henderson household had cancelled each other out. But what would the rest of the country say?

If my husband really cares about something, he cannot watch things unfold. Thinking back to our Durness holiday, he left the rest of us to cheer on Andy Murray at Wimbledon in the campsite bar while he took the dog for a long walk. 'He's going to lose, and that will wind me up,' he stated simply. He missed the Scot winning Wimbledon for the first time, a momentous moment for saltire waving, surely. On referendum night, he went to bed around midnight.

I found myself sitting in front of the television alone as the results rolled in. Who needs sleep – history was being made! It looked like the decision was on a knife-edge. When Glasgow backed independence by 55 per cent, I woke him up.

By the next morning, however, it was clear that the status quo was to continue. I had voted for this very outcome in order to stay in Europe but felt far from victorious. Flat, in fact. Rob, on the other hand, was bitterly disappointed. Over breakfast, my cautious, risk-averse and careful husband reflected: 'I'm surprised. I didn't think I'd feel this way.' Was the whole issue now settled for what First Minister Alex Salmond called 'a generation'?

If only things were this simple.

At a child's birthday party shortly afterwards, I had a chat with a father whom I knew very little. As usual, it didn't take long for talk of politics to emerge – my adopted home country had become exceedingly political over the past few months.

'Bloody foreigners lost us the referendum,' he grumbled. I didn't dare admit that I was one of them. 'And it's all the English, living here too. And the old people. It's their fault. They lost it for us.' Bitterness sprayed from every syllable.

Gosh. I didn't like this blame game, as if anyone who didn't agree with him had spoilt his party or deprived him of what was rightfully his.

I have often reflected on that day. Considering what followed with Brexit, I feel duped by the argument which swayed me at the time. Thinking of Covid and the resultant economic fallout, I wonder how we would have weathered such a storm alone. Am I still on the fence?

No. I'd vote differently this time.

Interestingly, the signs in my local drives and fields haven't disappeared.

Jana McNee – Czech Republic

As a Chartered Physiotherapist, Pilates instructor and mother of young children, Jana McNee certainly has her work cut out. The young woman's command of the English language is remarkable now, but her journey with Scotland started more than ten years ago when she met her Scottish husband back in the Czech Republic. 'He was the native speaker in my English class. Somehow, we managed to communicate,' she recalls with a smile, 'and he moved to the Czech Republic to be with me.'

The family relocated to Scotland four years ago because of a wider range of job opportunities for both Jana and her husband. Now she works in a physiotherapy and sports injury clinic in rural Perthshire. Since qualifying, Jana has completed several postgraduate courses to extend her skills, covering neck and back pain, muscle and joint injuries and sports injuries. She has pitch-side first aid qualifications, is training with the Australian Physiotherapy and Pilates Institution and is also working towards a sports massage qualification. However, having her degree recognised in Scotland proved a challenge for Jana. 'I obviously qualified back home, so I had to go through the process for my qualification to be recognised. It took about a year, actually.'

During the 2020 Coronavirus lockdown, Jana decided to run free online low-intensity workout classes for patients. 'It was something I could do; keep people connected, keep people moving – especially those who were shielding. I wanted to do something.' She also created online Pilates classes to raise money towards the charity Tayside Health Fund. 'We managed to raise £372 and it was used to provide toiletries and newspapers for hospital patients who were unable to have visitors due to Covid-19.'

Watching the run-up to the Brexit referendum of 2016 from Europe, the couple had hoped for a different outcome. 'Obviously we hoped that Britain would choose to stay in the EU. Brexit added some uncertainty to our situation, but it didn't change our decision to move to Scotland. We are still unsure about how things are going to develop and what Brexit will mean in practice, but so far it hasn't really affected us much where we live.'

Jana has pre-settled status and is considering applying for British citizenship. But that doesn't mean she is not trying to keep her Czech heritage alive. 'I try to speak my language to my children, although it is difficult. Our family traditions are a combination of Scottish and Czech traditions, especially at Christmas and Easter.'

She is grateful to Scotland for giving her family a home and showing her such a warm welcome. 'Working as a physio and with the children attending nursery and ballet, I have got to know my local community better. The best bit is when you walk down the street and someone waves and smiles and shouts "Hi, Jana!" – that's when you feel part of life here. You are known, and recognised, and that's lovely.'

26

Hands Up

*How wonderful it is that nobody need wait a single moment before
starting to improve the world.* – Anne Frank

MY PRIMARY SCHOOL needed parent helpers to run a school library. As
a book lover, that particular volunteering vacancy had my name on it!
I became part of a small team of enthusiastic librarians, echoing the
school library lunch hour I had covered all those years ago. As soon as
I was seated on my library days, the first class began to file out towards
me and disperse towards the bookshelves. I accepted returns, listening
to their views. Six-year-olds, take it from me, are the most opinionated
people on the planet. *Well, if you liked that book there, you might like
this one here.* I became a library tour guide, pointing out favourites and
classics. I really looked forward to these slots, especially once I had got
to know 'my' classes. I'd anticipate their antics and coax shy ones from
their shells. Occasionally, I gathered them all to introduce a new book
or present a selection of reads which tied in with their topic. Connecting
books and little people was my thing! And little people were much less
scary to me now than they had been at the after-school club all those
years ago.

Rob and I also began volunteering for the RSPB as helpers in their
Wildlife Explorers club. Looking back, it is one of the most memorable
and uplifting things I have ever done. It got us outside and engaging with
nature, and our whole family could be involved. I particularly loved when
our group visited the local bird ringers. A disused landfill site near the
football stadium had been abandoned and left to go wild. The volunteers
had stretched soft netting between the trees and the likeable man in charge
simply propped up his iPhone in the branches and pressed a button. A

high-pitched trill rang out.

'I'll try to get you a goldcrest' he smiled and we waited. Even the noisiest children in the group fell silent. Two or three bluetits and a blackbird were already wriggling in the net, but I was surprised how little the birds struggled once caught. They were obviously conserving their energy until an opportunity for escape presented itself. And then it happened – the tiniest flutter, the smallest streak of yellow. We were about to get a close-up look at Scotland's most miniscule bird. Carefully, we learned to close our hands gently around each trapped little creature, allowing a ring to be fixed around its leg and letting it fly free. They seemed to weigh nothing at all. The bluetits were, as a rule, vicious and their sharp beaks all but shredded my skin. But the goldcrest sat, resigned, on my daughter's palm and endured the procedure before soaring, singing, into the sky. It was a moment of shared joy, of connection, of privilege. How much of life and richness passes us by without our noticing? Our beautiful land screams 'notice me' with every sunset, seascape and flutter of tiny wings, with the ripple of sunlight on a cat's fur, with the dance of branches in the breeze. And we? We stare downwards at screens and reams of paper, listening to notifications and noise instead.

Look up. Listen. Learn. Lessons of this kind have stayed with me to this day.

I continued to write, of course, and I did have some small-scale successes with competitions, but the publication deal I had been craving proved elusive still. Even *Fir for Luck*, the clearances story I considered my best work, had so far sunk without a trace. The Kelpies Prize ceremony was a distant memory.

Nevertheless, my determination was growing.

'How long do you think you're going to keep trying?' asked my protective husband who had seen me rake in around 100 rejections from agents and publishers by then. I was stunned. I hadn't really considered giving up.

'Until it happens.' I shrugged.

Our younger daughter had joined a local basketball club and one of the by-products was a constant stream of basketball-related motivational quotes I gleaned along the way. 'The only way to guarantee never scoring is to stop taking the shots' was my favourite, pinned up above my desk.

Don't get me wrong, there were many moments of doubt – by then

I knew hundreds of writers whose first language was English and who had yet to break through into publishing. By anyone's standards, this was difficult. Who was I trying to kid? But in my more lucid moments I remembered the 'nearlies', the 'almost theres' and the phrase which echoed in my ears whenever anything was difficult. 'Why ever not?'

True, I wasn't a published writer yet, but surely, I could put myself into the best possible situation for when it eventually happened – which it would, of course. I tried to convince myself rather than anyone else. I set to work. World Book Day was approaching, and even if I wasn't a published children's writer, I was a school librarian. 'Do you want me to organise some activities for World Book Day?' I asked the Head Teacher, and she was only too glad to outsource that particular responsibility. I set to work on creating a skeleton script for a Blind Date with a Book show, improvised and complete with screen to separate the would-be-reader from three contestants who were each answering questions on behalf of the book in their hands. I had even recorded the Blind Date theme tune to play in between rounds. It was a success – my gamble had paid off. Step two – begin a blog.

As a self-confessed technophobe who detested social media and even balked at emails, this was a big undertaking, but the free templates soon resulted in regular posts – I had an internet presence, just in case this should matter to agents and publishers. Good, good! Next on my list was changing my approach. The old adage goes: *If you do what you've always done, you'll get what you've always got.* Something had to change. Once more, I approached the local school. 'Hi there – you probably know that I've been writing children's stories. Well. I would like to write one from scratch and read it to the kids as I write it, say once a week? Would you be up for that?'

In a flash, I was assigned two primary six classes on a Friday afternoon. I committed to reading them three new chapters every week. It was terrifying, but that manuscript practically wrote itself. Every Friday, I arrived with a giant water bottle and a pack of post-it notes. Every week, the pupils would give their honest, often brutal views on what I had written, as soon as they heard it. I soon discovered what worked and what didn't. It was a light-hearted story about children and dogs with a crime mystery woven in. There were paragraphs which I had considered pure genius before realising: when kids fiddle with their pencil cases, they are probably bored. A wee sentence which I had thought only mildly amusing reduced 60 children to tears of laughter, with some of them still giggling when I finished half an hour later.

It was a steep, steep learning curve and I blogged about every turn of events under the heading 'The Experiment'. But the most memorable moment of that initiative did not even take place in the classroom. It took place at the traffic crossing outside the baker's shop. I was waiting to cross with my dog when I felt a tugging at my sleeve. I looked down. A small, bespectacled child looked up at me. I only vaguely recognised him. 60 children sort of blend into one when they are all wearing the same uniform.

'You're my favourite author, you know,' the kid said simply before crossing and going on his way, leaving me welling up. To this child, I was an author. He knew little of the publishing game: the pitches and submissions and the many rejections. But he was an expert at confidence building. That kid said I'm an author – and who was I to argue with him?

My steps home were a little bouncier and my smile a little easier as I prepared to press 'send' again. Surely, surely, this time...

It didn't work. Another fistful of rejections for *The Dog Walking Consortium* rained into my inbox and onto my party. But I did win two writing competitions in 2015, one of them a US-based international one. *Take heart Barbara. The only way you guarantee never scoring...*

Social media was the only bastion I hadn't attempted to conquer. I wasn't on Facebook, Instagram or Twitter. I'd been the last of my friends to even get a smartphone. I resented the thought of 'being out there' – wasn't my wee blog enough? *If you do what you've always done, you'll get what you've always got.*

I reluctantly joined Facebook and connected with relevant writers' groups. And why stop there? My local arts festival, XpoNorth had advertised a Twitter pitching event for the beginning of the new year – 'New year, new start. Pitch your writing to the Scottish publishing scene by using the hashtag...'

With a day or so to spare, I signed up for an account and honed my seven unpublished children's books into hopefully compelling Twitter pitches. I could always delete my account afterwards, couldn't I?

My first tweet of the day went something like this:

Scotland, 1842. Janet (12) stands alone between her village and the eviction writ. She chooses to fight. Cue riots, regiments and ruin.

It didn't take long before someone responded. Someone I had never heard of.

'Who on earth is Cranachan Publishing?' I asked organisers of the pitching event. 'And what do I do if someone likes the tweet?'

'Ah, a *like* is a tentative expression of interest. Look them up and ask if they'd like to see a submission from you.'

I googled the company's website, which was still under construction, with the familiar Latin holding text. Were they even ready? I asked around. No, these guys were genuine new kids on the block. What did I have to lose? I emailed a carefully worded enquiry and submitted my work, submission 122 on my huge spreadsheet. Fingers crossed, but I had been at the 'nearly' stage too often to invest much of myself. Normally publishers took months to get back to you anyway, and many never answered at all. I poured my efforts into another writing project. I was astounded when I received an answer within days.

'Dear Barbara. We have read the first three chapters of *Fir for Luck* and love the story so far. If you have finished the manuscript, we'd love to read the rest of it.'

This was good news, I guess. I fired off the rest of the manuscript and the hoping began. But I was also wary. Apocryphal tales of writers being fleeced of their cash abound in writing circles. Scam publishers often take advantage of the hopes and dreams of aspiring writers. Was I about to fall into one of those traps?

'Ask around some more,' suggested Rob, my ever-cautious husband. 'Someone is bound to know something.'

But jinx it before I had been offered anything at all? No, I'd wait.

I didn't have to wait long. A few days later I received an email:

Dear Barbara. All of us have now read your book *Fir for Luck* and we would very much like to meet you to discuss working together.

The lines blurred a little. They wanted to meet me! That didn't smack of a business trying to hide something. I so badly wanted to be happy and just enjoy the breakthrough I had waited for so long, but I worried about being naïve.

I rang a literary agent who had rejected every single one of my manuscripts for advice. She wasn't one to mince her words, I knew that from bitter experience, and there was nothing in the Scottish publishing scene she didn't know. In fact, I'd wager there was little in any publishing scene she didn't know. She had seen my work, and after all, I was only asking for five minutes of her time. Luck favours the brave, right?

To her eternal credit, she didn't dismiss me out of hand. If she was perplexed that I had rung her out of the blue when I wasn't even her client, she didn't show it. 'Sounds like it may be worth a shot,' she concluded after listening patiently. 'If they ask for any money, be on your guard. But all of the Scottish publishers started small. And you haven't got that many other options.'

Ouch.

But my mind was made up. The fact that the publishers were willing to travel from Glasgow and from the Isle of Lewis just to meet me was incredible in itself. They named a restaurant in Inverness and on 11 February 2016, I set off on my short walk across the river to meet the team behind Cranachan Publishing. Excitement and nervousness rose with every step. They liked the manuscript. But would they like me? How could I convince them to take a chance on me? My German-ness hung around my head like a giant sign. I probably wasn't the sort of poster girl they'd want for their explicitly Scottish brand.

It turned out that I wasn't the only one who had prepared to convince at that meeting. The lady called Helen held up sample designs and promotion plans.

'We know we are new and a bit of a risk for you,' Cranachan's managing director Anne said, 'but this is what we can offer.'

Their business plan sounded like a great fit for my writing – an emphasis on the schools' market, with bookshops and the general reader in mind too. They even had plans to create integrated teaching materials alongside each book. They wanted to foster a personal, family feel to the publishing company. Clan Cranachan.

We clinked glasses. *Fir for Luck* was going to be a real book. A BOOK! And as soon as the following September. I could barely believe it. My German accent wasn't mentioned once. Not once.

I floated home. On the kitchen table, a huge bunch of flowers, a bottle of champagne and a congratulations card signed thoughtfully by Rob and the kids waited for me.

'How did you know it was going to work out?' I asked him.

'I had faith in you,' he answered with a grin. 'Although if the door had opened slowly and you'd slouched in, I figured I'd have enough time to shove it all into a cupboard.'

Thomas Farrugia – Malta

'So, what do you do?' First Minister Nicola Sturgeon asked the entrepreneur Thomas Farrugia at a reception for innovators at Bute House.

'I create better bugs,' answered the young geneticist without batting an eyelid. There was a semi-awkward pause before conversation moved on. As the First Minister walked away, she told him: 'Stay crazy!'

Fist-bumping Scotland's top politician aside, the scientist from Malta has had his fair share of high points since moving to Scotland, albeit via London and Bristol. Now based at Midlothian's Roslin Innovation Centre, his company Beta Bugs accelerate insect evolution, creating new breeds of commercially farmed insects for the alternative protein industry in order to drive a sustainable bio-economy. Put simply, he is in the business of manipulating the genetic composition of the black soldier fly to create high-performance breeds.

Thomas was announced as a Royal Society of Edinburgh (RSE) Unlocking Ambition Enterprise Fellow in 2018, and his entrepreneurial start-up is hosted at the prestigious centre as a result. He employs a small workforce, and his research ensures that Scotland is at the forefront of a new, rapidly growing industry.

'Scotland is progressive and innovative. There is a lot to do,' he enthuses about the country he now calls home. 'Even the weather isn't quite as bad as I expected!' He is gradually getting used to the way society is structured and to the political systems here. 'Both Malta and Scotland are home now,' he states. 'Malta is home, where my family and my old friends are. But there are more opportunities here in Scotland. It's why I came. I do bake my own bread though – what you have here isn't bread, really!' Farrugia's home baking includes the traditional Maltese Easter Figolli biscuits, a fleeting flavour of home.

Endearingly, Thomas intersperses his talk with Scots phrases: 'People in Edinburgh talk to you on the bus – you can have a wee bit of a blether.' It is clear that he values the city of Edinburgh, its beauty and its history – but he also speaks with raw enthusiasm about ceilidhs, mountain biking and the wild landscape of the Isle of Bute. 'The sheer variety of the terrain is striking, and the fact that the days up north are so long.'

All of this feels a long way away removed from Bristol where he was based during the Brexit referendum of 2016. 'I have a really clear memory of referendum day. It was a sunny day there. My flat was on the top floor and I looked down onto the street where a car was driving past, with Union Jack flags fluttering from the windows and blaring out *Rule Britannia*. By the next day, it had happened.' Farrugia is still forming a view on where he sees Scotland's best future, as part of the UK or on its own. 'Scotland is doing its own thing, which is great. But could we be in the EU again if we went for independence? I'm not sure yet.' But he does not hesitate when asked what he would tell Scotland.

He laughs. 'Nae bother! Excel at your strengths; be true to yourself. And above all, stay crazy!'

SCOTTISH BY INCLINATION

27

The Brexit Referendum

A day will come when you — France, Russia, Italy, England,
Germany — all you nations of the continent will merge, without
losing your distinct qualities and your glorious individuality, in a close
and higher unity to form a European brotherhood. – Victor Hugo

THE JUNE MORNING sun swirled through the glass. I fumbled to switch off my alarm and blinked hard before swinging myself out of bed. As the only early riser in our family (and even that label is worn half-heartedly), I staggered downstairs and clipped the dog on the lead. The morning dog-walks are mine, generally. In the evening, I wilt like a daisy and the thought of heading out into the inevitable lashing rain fills me with dread. No, I'd rather take the morning hit. There are a variety of routes around our neighbourhood in Inverness. It becomes an autopilot exercise. Except for that morning.

'Hello,' shouted a man from two streets along. 'Big day today, huh?'

My brain was still doing its morning stretches. 'What? Why big day?'

'Brexit!' He shook his head. He was a fellow German, a forester who had lived here almost as long as I had. His wife had taken their child to our German group years ago. 'Aren't you worried?' he wanted to know.

Why would I be worried? I didn't think I knew a single person who supported Brexit and surely Nigel Farage by himself couldn't win a referendum.

'No. Not worried,' I declared blithely.

'Ahh,' he answered with his trademark smile. 'I'm not so sure.'

I walked home more slowly than I had set out. Really? Was it even remotely possible that the country would vote to come out of Europe? The pictures of endless lines of Eastern Europeans queuing up to get into

Britain had been discredited. The £300 million a week for the NHS claim had been a fabrication of the Leave campaign. No, I thought, people can see through this. And yet...

I watched Invernessians stand in line outside the polling station at the end of our road, but I didn't join them. As a European citizen I had no right to vote in a UK referendum. That in itself was unsettling – as EU citizens here, we were the ones whose lives would be most drastically affected, and yet on this issue, we were silenced. I had no voice in the decision the country would make that day. I valued the institution immensely: the EU had made free movement possible for people like me, enabling us to work, live and study wherever we chose. Now I had to trust those around me to value it too. And I did.

In the run-up to the day, it was hard not to take some of the debate personally. Several acquaintances had expressed surprise that this referendum had anything to do with me. 'We don't mean you, obviously. Not people like you.'

People like me who lived and worked here, claimed no benefits and contributed to society by volunteering and looking after their local communities? Well, that was a little rich. The point was, if we left the EU, people like me wouldn't be able to come in the first place! Of course, I recognise that not every person who supported Brexit had a personal vendetta against immigrants, but in the rhetoric, it felt like a driving factor.

In the evening, there was a real sense of occasion on the BBC.

'Polls have now closed for the referendum on Britain's membership of the European Union,' announced David Dimbleby, the veteran journalist who, entertainingly, had to miss *Question Time* once because he had been knocked unconscious by a bull on his Sussex farm. 'We expect the first results to come in at midnight.'

Rob and I exchanged a glance across the sofa.

'Are we staying up?' I asked. Rob hesitated. It was a Thursday, a school night. He'd have work the next morning.

'For a bit,' he mumbled. The unspoken words hung in the air. *We'll watch until we're sure that there is nothing to worry about. We'll soon see how it's going.*

We brewed some strong coffee, gently coaxed the teenagers upstairs and made ourselves comfortable. I brought a duvet down from the bedroom.

There was much speculation. Interviews with focus groups and interested commentators only part-held our interest. The footage of students sprinting across sports halls with ballot boxes was more like it. It felt like a Hollywood blockbuster, and hopefully one which was going to finish with a satisfying outcome. We expected to be safe, in a rollercoaster sort of way. You take your seat and strap in. For a moment, the illusion of deadly danger sends your heart rate soaring. But you're never in danger – not really.

We began to shift uncomfortably as result after result was shared. True to my expectation, Scotland voted comfortably to stay within the European Union, but it was a different story in England. At around one o'clock, Rob decided to go to bed.

'I can't watch anymore,' he said. I stretched myself out on my own and wrapped the duvet tightly around me for comfort as I saw the world I knew crumble. Had I ever known this country at all? Who were these people who wanted to stop immigration at all cost? Who around me had been in on the plan? I drifted in and out of the nightmare. At 4.40am on 24 June 2016, a tired looking David Dimbleby announced: 'The British people have spoken, and their answer is: we're out!'

I woke Rob to let him know. A couple more hours of sleep were wishful thinking.

The days which followed were a strange blur, a hangover of scrambled thoughts and tearfulness. I was mortified to find myself crying on an elevator in the local shopping centre. *Who of you voted for this?* I wondered as I looked across the throng of shoppers. *We don't mean you? Not people like you? It's not personal?*

From where I was standing, the decision felt very personal indeed.

Lina Langlee – Sweden

When literary agent Lina Langlee first moved to Scotland to study in 2008, she packed warm and sensible clothes. She expected to sit in cafés, watching the rain beat against the window while reading books. 'I should have brought my dancing shoes instead!' she jokes. Scotland swiftly had her in its spell: 'I fell in love with the people, with the landscape and with the atmosphere,' she enthuses. 'I spent my formative 20s here, building friendships, breaking into the industry I wanted to work in, meeting my now husband. He proposed to me at Neist Point on Skye – it was exactly the Scotland of my imagination, wild, rugged and perfectly beautiful.'

Lina is based in Edinburgh and values the buzz of the festival city. 'I love the Edinburgh International Book Festival where you can listen to speakers who make you think and feel like you have a personal epiphany about something – and then you can head to the Fringe, grab some street food and make for the dance floor. Scotland is that mix of inspiration and a willingness to always have a great time – people here don't take themselves too seriously, but they are fiercely proud to be Scottish.'

Does she feel Scottish? 'Yes, but I also feel Swedish, and firmly believe you can be both. I've absolutely developed that Scottish chip on my shoulder and feel incapable not to correct someone if they say "England" when they, in fact, mean the UK.'

The first time Lina felt acutely like a foreigner was the morning after the Brexit referendum in 2016. She remembers boarding a bus, wondering how her fellow travellers had voted. 'Did they know what this meant for me? Did they know how personal it was?' She has applied for settled status but not for citizenship. 'It's a very personal protest which benefits no one and might even harm me,' she laughs. 'But at the moment I can't face jumping through hoops to get that blue passport.'

Professionally, Lina Langlee is understatedly proud of what she does. 'I am particularly pleased to be working in Scotland when so much of the publishing industry is London-centric. I hope it sets an example for others. My work also very much involves helping others achieve their dreams – what an honour that is!'

When asked about her contribution to Scottish society, the discussion turns to whether an immigrant should have to make more of a contribution than someone who is Scottish by birth. 'At the moment, I'd say I'm like any Scottish person who is doing pretty well for themselves and who hasn't fallen on any hardship. I work, pay my taxes and my mortgage and get on with life. Should I need to do more?' Lina acknowledges that not everyone's immigration story is as seamless as hers: 'I blend in here, visually and culturally speaking, and I have never felt unwelcome. But that is not everyone's experience. In fact, plenty of British people will have experienced more xenophobia than I have, despite being born here.'

However, she is optimistic about Scotland's place in the world. 'While we're not always in line with UK policies, Scotland's views and my own tend to align. I come from a small country and believe small countries can punch well beyond their weight. Having an international outlook is good not only for the heart and mind, but also the purse.' She adds: 'I want to be here. I am not only Scottish by inclination; I am Scottish by choice.'

28

The Season of Favour

Autumn is a second spring when every leaf is a flower. – Albert Camus

IT HAD BEEN a tricky summer, but things were looking up.

In February, I had tweeted: 'So gutted Inverness doesn't have a book festival anymore. Anyone want to help me make this happen?' By August, we had a constitution, a committee and a plan. We were going to run an autumn book festival. Now, the sensible approach would have been to take our time and schedule a festival a year ahead to plan for every eventuality. Instead, our overenthusiastic bunch of NessBookFest volunteers decided to organise a book festival from a standing start in little more than eight weeks. It was remarkable and the festival has gone strong ever since.

It wasn't the only significant thing which happened that autumn. Yes, I was still reeling from the Brexit referendum result, but there was good news in town too: I was, finally, to be a published author. I will never ever forget the day my copies arrived in the post, real books with a tactile, soft finish on the paper. The cover showed a half-face with fire reflected in the eye. It was effective, it was compelling and best of all, it had my name on it. My name was on an actual book.

A German newspaper had made contact. 'We'd like to publish a feature on you. Can you take a picture with the book, in front of the location you use as your setting?' I explained that Durness was more than three hours' drive away, so I cheated, posing on a very windy afternoon on Culloden Battlefield. It would have to do.

Now, time to get organised for an actual book launch.

My morning was spent in the very school where my children had been pupils and I had been a volunteer librarian. Talking to a full assembly, I alternated activities and drama games with a presentation about what had inspired the book. I was a familiar face to so many, and yet today felt different. Many of the pupils had brought money to buy a signed copy of *Fir for Luck* and I lingered long in the hall, signing at speed in increasingly messy handwriting – my first signed copies! We ran home to make the lunchtime edition of the radio news for the Highlands and Islands which contained a snippet of an interview I had recorded at the BBC studio the previous evening. That, too, felt surreal. A quick lunch, and we were back in preparation mode, this time for the public event at my local Waterstones bookshop.

'Oh my goodness, oh my goodness, oh wow, wow,' gasped Anne, Cranachan's managing director, as we headed down the hill towards the launch venue. Her phone had pinged with a message from her husband. *Check Amazon,* it said. 'Oh wow, wow, wow…' She waved a screenshot in my face. It took me some time to compute the fact that my book, my wee debut published that day, had reached Number One in its category. In my wildest dreams I couldn't have dreamt of that. What better start could a new author wish for?

Waterstones Inverness had ordered in 70 copies of *Fir for Luck*, but I had brought an extra bag of more books from home, just in case.

Helen (who was chairing the event) and I took our seats at the front and exchanged a glance of pure buzz. We had come a long way since clinking glasses at the restaurant in February. Just as well that I had brought extra book supplies! Every single copy sold, and most of mine too – more than a hundred people squeezed into the upper floor of the bookshop in the Eastgate shopping centre, and people were queuing all the way down the stairs. I stood up to give my first reading, amplified across the shop by the microphones. Words I had written.

'Weren't you nervous?' a friend asked afterwards.

'Not really, once I got going,' I answered truthfully. The whole evening was one of excitement and buzz. I had been waiting for this for years. To share the story which had occupied my mind for so long. To see young people care about what happened to my characters. Days later, I revisited the school to deliver more books to a few stragglers. The plan was for individual pupils to come out of class. I signed their books in the corridor before returning them to their lessons.

'What's your name?' I asked the little girl with curly hair who was first in the queue of two. I signed a copy of *Fir for Luck* to her, adding my usual quote: 'Be a force for good', and handed her the book. Her friend was next. Once finished, the two huddled away towards their class together, the curly-haired girl stretching her arm out ahead of her. 'The author touched my hand,' she squeaked excitedly, skipping through the door as if I was some sort of rock star.

Days later, I found myself on the road north. Hills, lochans and windswept crags flew by to the tune of folk music. I was beginning to live my dream: this was the day of my very first school author visit. I hoped there would be many more. It seemed fitting that this visit would take me to the charming little Durness Primary School, local to Ceannabeinne. The pupils showed me the beautiful tapestry the community had created of the incident which sparked my imagination. Despite their low school roll, the tiny school bought several copies of the book. I glanced out through the window anxiously as I explained the inspiration behind the story and the research I had done. The main part of the visit was still to come. I had hoped to be able to take the small group of children to the actual site, the Ceannabeinne Clearance Trail where it all began for me. And hooray, the sun made an appearance – it was windy, but definitely doable. We travelled in two cars. Within minutes we were standing where I had stood years before and discovered this story for the very first time. It was every bit as majestic, albeit a little colder in early October.

I handed out costumes, wigs and props. Being a Drama teacher has its advantages: I had raided the costume cupboard for the purpose. I led the children to the ruin of the very house where I had imagined Janet, my main character, living. I read loudly enough to let my voice carry over the wind, and just as in my book, the waves rolled in like a heartbeat, steady and strong. I don't think I have ever felt a stronger connection with the land and its story. It didn't matter where I came from. I was here. Just like these children, dressed in ludicrous tartan and grotesque granny wigs, I belonged. The land's heartbeat was ours.

We laughed a lot as we made our way to one of the highest points, the children's oversized kilts fluttering around their bodies like whips. 'Hold on to your hats' I shouted, but it was too late – a flat-cap I had only bought from a charity shop the day before soared high into the air before being sucked over the cliff-edge in a single jerky movement. We could hear the waves pounding rocks beneath. The mortified little boy in question made to sprint to the edge.

'STOP,' I yelled. 'It's not worth it. Don't worry about it.'

We hurriedly took group photos for the school and headed back down the hill again, this time to re-enact throwing stones, just as the villagers had done to keep the superintendent and his writ away.

It was a picture-book-day of screaming seabirds, lively breeze, blue skies and bluer waters. The young people I met that day responded with genuine excitement to my wee book. My first author visit had gone well.

It's a wonder that my car did not take off on the way home, so sky-high were my spirits!

Maria de la Torre – Spain

Spanish environmental lawyer Maria de la Torre is a force of nature. Now employed by NatureScot (formerly Scottish Natural Heritage), she arrived in Aberdeen for a year-long Master's degree in Environmental Law. 'In the beginning I felt very foreign. You constantly say the wrong thing or get your times wrong. In Spain, if someone invites you to a party, you turn up at 10.00pm. Here people start leaving by then. It makes you feel inadequate, so to start with I was almost counting the days until I could return to Spain. But by the end of the year I had adjusted, made friends and was enjoying the hills. I got married and had children. All of these things create roots.'

Her job with the conservation body is an advisory role where her legal and policy expertise is sought on agricultural and environmental schemes. She sighs when I ask about her perspective on Brexit: 'Much of what we do is connected to the Common Agricultural Policy which will be directly affected by our departure from the EU,' she says. 'Our strength is working with our partners across the UK and the EU, to share experience and knowledge. The political rhetoric in Westminster simply doesn't reflect what is going on at an institutional level. We are still collaborating while being told not to. The door is closing. I have taught European Environmental Law – the fact is that we have spent the last 20 years unifying our approaches and sorting out legal differences. From a conservation institution's point of view, Brexit is a huge step backwards!'

The natural world has played a fundamental part in Maria's relationship with Scotland. A keen hillwalker and mountaineer, she soon found like-minded people. 'The hills brought me my connections here,' she muses. 'I remember the first harsh winters here with snow on the hills. When you're out in that kind of landscape, you feel part of the same thing. It didn't matter where anyone came from, because that shared passion for the hills had brought us together.'

Her Spanish identity is still strong, with lengthy and regular family visits to Spain and a bilingual household. 'There are two parts to me. But I am still to apply for settled status. Emotionally and professionally, Brexit is just so unnecessary, and such a hassle! I wish I had campaigned more in the run-up to it, but I felt disenfranchised, because I had no vote in it. There should have been legal challenges about the validity of how things were done. It is a regret.'

Maria did organise a public pro-EU rally in Inverness in the aftermath of the referendum, but her disillusionment with the political process has not dampened her appetite for activism – she is the chairperson of her local community council and is also instrumental in a campaign to save a local plot of land from commercial development. The vision is to turn it into an allotment site with a community education and business function. 'It's government-owned land, so we should make the case for it to be used in a beneficial way. It echoes the government's priorities on food, health and education, and we have just received a grant to progress the project.'

Is she ever tempted to stand back and let other people fight the battles?

'I suppose I want to make a difference; I can't help myself.' She pauses before giggling: 'Sometimes I wish I wasn't bothered, but I am.'

29

Mad March

A man does not seek his luck; luck seeks its man. – Turkish proverb

'FLIPPING SPAM!'

I hovered my mouse over the strange message. Someone was surely trying to wind me up.

'Hello Barbara, I work for a Turkish TV station and would like to interview you. We are going to do a feature on World Book Day and wondered if we could speak to you in relation to it.'

I was about to click on the delete button. But World Book Day was indeed coming up. The email signature looked professional enough, and their website oozed kudos too. If this message was genuine, what on earth had possessed them to get in touch with me, of all people?

I tentatively worded a reply along the lines of 'Hello, I'm very honoured that you should want to talk to me in connection with World Book Day, and of course I'd be willing. However, I am not a very famous author and there are probably others who are more experienced...' You get the idea.

The answer came swiftly. 'Great. It is you we wanted to get in touch with,' the emailer insisted. 'We'd like to ask you some questions about World Book Day.'

'Could you tell me a little bit more about what is involved?' I typed back.

The researcher at the other end replied with details of Turkey's English language news channel and its flagship cultural programme, *Showcase*, hosted by television presenter Özlem Işiten. I was none the wiser.

'All right. Yes, I'd be happy to be interviewed by you.'

And thus began the most surreal episode of my author life to date.

By return email I received a range of instructions: Skype contact rules, timings, soundchecks.

Could I place the computer at face level?

I ran for a pile of books.

Could the background be a little less cluttered?

I speed-spring-cleaned my kitchen, placing my book covers – by then there were two – strategically on the dresser.

Could I speak up a little? Great. 'Stay on the line; we'll be recording in a minute.'

Oh my word! Were they not even going to tell me the questions ahead of time? I panicked, brushed my hair, flung mascara at my deadly pale eyes and grabbed a slightly more decorative scarf to liven up my boring T-shirt.

'Don't worry Barbara, it'll be really informal,' the friendly researcher assured me. I took a deep breath. The dramatic theme tune began to play, and a voice spoke: 'What's the aim of World Book Day and what does it mean to children around the world?'

The word 'fantastic' featured a lot in my answer. Couldn't I vary it up a little more? At least I managed to squeeze in something about inspiring the next generation to read. I mentioned authors visiting schools and museums and bridging the gap between young readers and the people who create the books that they had in their hands. So far so good.

She asked what kids actually did on World Book Day. This was safer territory. 'So, it completely varies from case to case.' I explained what my own author visits would normally entail. I listed dressing up as book characters and decorating common spaces, but like a virus, the word 'fantastic' popped up again. It was embarrassing.

'But does World Book Day actually encourage children to read more?'

How should I know? What were they expecting here, statistics? But I was here as the expert, so I'd better pretend to know. 'I think...'

Considering I hadn't expected this, it didn't go too badly, listing all the positive experiences which children could connect with reading, even if I didn't exactly answer the question. Best of all, I managed to avoid saying 'fantastic' again, opting instead for 'awesome' which was probably even more cringeworthy.

I also talked about Scotland and how World Book Day was celebrated here. I am sure there were many repetitions and hesitations. Surely, they would edit those out, or let me re-record some of what I said?

'Perfect!' said the voice at the other end of the Skype call resolutely.

The interview aired on World Book Day itself. I was busy visiting a school, but I managed to track down the recording on the TRT World YouTube channel:

In celebration of World Book Day, *Showcase* spoke to Scottish author Barbara Henderson. We look into the importance of the day and how it is commemorated by children around the world. Henderson writes children's fiction and her latest book, *Punch*, was released last October.

Guilt washed over me. They hadn't explicitly asked my nationality. I had forgotten to mention it. And now it was too late. The programme had gone out. Had I lied, implicitly? Had I done wrong? I agonised before remembering the slogan I had heard on TV. *Scottish by inclination.* Perhaps I wasn't an imposter. I wrote books in one of the languages of Scotland, about Scottish history, published by a Scottish publisher. The books were widely studied in Scottish schools. I had lived in Scotland for more than a quarter of a century. I had Scottish children, a Scottish husband and I had answered my interview questions in fluent English with a Scottish accent.

Enough, I decided.

If someone wants to call me a Scottish author, I will let them.

It was a liberating thought.

* * *

That same month, I got a phone call.

'Barbara, are you free to come on Saturday?'

I didn't know the woman on the other end of the line well, although I had been aware of Maria for some years. Our children had attended traditional music classes together and we were often standing in the corridor together, waiting for the lesson to finish.

'It's the 60th anniversary of the Treaty of Rome and I'm trying to organise this pro-EU protest, but I could do with some help.' Maria oozes competence. The Spanish academic had often communicated useful information to us unsettled Europeans in the Highlands in the wake of the European Union referendum. The Scottish government had held support meetings to reassure us all that we were wanted and would receive help through the process. One such meeting featured our local MP who talked about the myriad ways in which the government would seek to help us. But it was Maria who piped up at the end and asked those willing to connect to share their email addresses, and who recommended helpful social media sites to the 50 or so Highland Europeans who, like me, were trying to get their heads around what all of this meant for them and their families.

Now, a few months later, she was taking the initiative again.

'I could do with a bit of help with the publicity, Barbara. You're a writer, aren't you?'

I began to draft press releases. The discourse in the political arena was particularly odious at that time – the EU negotiators had offered to protect the rights of British citizens living in the EU, but the British government refused to do the same in return, preferring to hold that particular card for a later date. I was personally enraged. I had been a taxpayer all my professional life, I hadn't relied on benefits and I felt reduced to a bargaining chip. It was the perfect mindset for a protest.

Unrolling a large piece of card, I used my children's years-old lumpy paint to make my point:

26 years in the UK.

Taxpayer

Wife

Mother

Teacher

Volunteer

Bargaining Chip

The protest fell on a Saturday. My nephew from Germany was visiting at the time and was promptly roped in too. We carried our banners down the Market Stairs towards Falcon Square, Inverness's focal point. The statue of Scotland's emblematic unicorn gleamed in the crisp sunlight as we assembled around it. It wasn't a large protest. The Scottish way is not to draw attention to yourself and to keep your head down. After nearly three decades here, that has rubbed off a little. Many voices, including my own heart at times, would convince me not to write this book, not to stick my head above the parapet. And wasn't it too late to make the point now that the referendum decision had been made and that negotiations about the leaving process were underway?

No, we argued. It wasn't too late to make the strength of our feelings known and to emphasise that we as Europeans among you felt strongly about the unity among nations that had enabled us to be here in the first place. I still immensely value the friendship shown by those who turned up to stand with me on that day. They were willing to be counted and to stand with me, to state clearly that they valued Europeans like me among them.

It was a little awkward, yes. I am not in the habit of protesting, and I was a little uneasy with other protesters' signs claiming boldly 'We won't leave the EU!' when I knew that that ship had sailed. But it was emotional too, like a final stand of a retreating army. Not ashamed, no. But ready to run. I felt a strange mix of emotions. On the one hand, I was surrounded by acquaintances and strangers who knew exactly how it felt to be suddenly cast into such uncertainty. On the other hand, there were those who cared enough to be part of it, for our sake.

And decisions, which had not been necessary before, now needed to be made.

Settled status? Citizenship? Relocation? Paperwork and documentation. Proof.

I badly wanted to bury my head in the sand and pretend none of this was happening, and for a while, that is exactly what I did.

Kristian Tapaninaho is the Finnish-born co-founder of the fastest growing private business in Scotland, outdoor pizza oven manufacturer Ooni. The entrepreneur who runs the company with his wife Darina Garland from Ooni's headquarters in Broxburn, moved both family and business to Scotland in 2014. It was the immediate aftermath of the independence referendum. 'I am in the process of applying for British citizenship now – it'll make it easier to run a business here and I don't resent it – but I've always joked I'd prefer to have a Scottish passport,' he laughs. 'I love the connection with nature up here, the fact there is just more space. With my wife from Scotland, it was the obvious choice.'

He hails from Pyhäsalmi, a small Finnish town, the boundaries of which are comparable to Greater London, but with only 5,000 inhabitants. 'Scotland and Finland are culturally more aligned, though I loved London too. The business community here has made us feel very welcome.'

The company's pre-Covid sales grew by an average of 148 per cent a year, reaching £10m in 2019, with sales in over 90 countries. Tapaninaho appreciates the support small businesses receive both from government and each other in Scotland and credits the move north of the border with his company's growth. 'We were a start-up, a bit of an outlier, but early-stage support meant that we weren't doing this alone. We expanded and were able to afford warehouse space outside Edinburgh. Now the *Times* has named us the seventh fastest growing company in the UK and the fastest in Scotland, and we try to do our part. We want to build a great workplace and take care of our employees by creating sustainable jobs – and by staying profitable so that those jobs remain secure.'

He does not mince his words when speaking about Brexit which he calls 'a disgrace': 'EU immigrants like me love this country and want it to succeed. Many are huge net contributors to the economy here and contribute more than the average Brit. The Leave campaign won on the basis of the *stop immigration* message, but really, there are not many economic arguments to support Brexit. As a businessman, it's just counterintuitive.'

Tapaninaho relishes the responsibility of citizenship. 'One of the things I am most looking forward to about having a British passport is being allowed to vote and make my voice heard.' But the vision for his business is bigger than that. One per cent of the company's annual turnover is invested back in projects like tree-planting in Madagascar (to offset the environmental impact of the ovens), and in social global emergency responses, for example in the Yemen or combating wildfires in the US.

Does he see himself as a global citizen?

'Yes,' he nods thoughtfully. 'I suppose I am.'

SCOTTISH BY INCLINATION

30

The Struggle to Settle

All for settling down. Not down for settling. There is a difference.
– Anonymous

IT WAS A short video, attached to a Home Office tweet.

'EU citizens and their families will need to apply to the EU Settlement Scheme to continue living in the UK after 31 December 2020,' it announced.

It is a convenient time, that little window between Christmas and New Year. The perfect time to bury controversial announcements. Nobody will care.

Applying for settled status had been very much on my mind. I had briefly considered applying for citizenship to put my presence here beyond all doubt, but continued uncertainty over the rights of EU citizens living abroad was still being debated at political level and the goalposts were constantly shifting. In any case, the financial cost of becoming a British citizen horrified me – one of the highest charges in the world. In a state of paralysis, I decided to wait for this new thing called 'settled status' even though the whole concept really irked me – it felt wrong to suddenly have to ask permission to stay with my family; to set myself apart again.

All of this I could have swallowed if it hadn't been for this particular Home Office tweet.

The video which accompanied it was a montage of text about the ease of application and stock photographs of smiling, deliriously happy, young and beautiful people. It was clear that there was nothing they would rather do than obtain settled status from a government who had refused to guarantee their rights and used them as bargaining chips. It went something like this:

An inviting outdoor restaurant table with glasses of beer and a diverse group of five 20-somethings seated around it, having fun. The text ran:

> If you are an EU citizen living in the UK, and want to stay in the UK after the 31st of December 2020, you and your family need to apply to the EU Settlement Scheme.

The picture had shifted to a young woman and her interested child, reading a book together and laughing. The upbeat music built up a little.

> Getting status under the scheme means you can continue to live, work and study in the UK as you can now.

The image had moved to a split screen of a cheerful waiter and three young people leaning onto a pub bar in uproarious laughter. Everyone looked like a film star and the pictures were separated by a lightning-shaped line.

> We're making the application process as quick and easy as possible.

A helpful, smiling woman wearing glasses seemed to be explaining something to a blond man concentrating gratefully. The diversity of the groups struck me. This was a government keen to look representative, but the same pictures were later discovered to be featured in other adverts around the globe. They were mere stock photos selected for the purpose of making settled status look accessible and, dare I say it, fun.

More text filled the screen:

> It will check three basic principles:
> 1. Identity.
> 2. Residence in the UK.
> 3. And criminality. The system is currently being tested and will be open fully by 30th March 2019.

The shot behind these words was a blurred crowd in a busy street, an attractive patchwork of colour and vitality. It seemed like a celebration of the mingling of cultures when Brexit itself was such a clear statement against all of that. The picture-book images really rankled now, amplified by the upbeat keyboard soundtrack.

The image shifted to a smiling young father, squinting against the bright sunlight and carrying his blonde, attractive child with perfectly styled hair through a decorated London Street.

It will cost £65 to apply, and £32.50 for children under 16

the Home Office assured us all.

It will be free to apply if you already have a valid indefinite leave to remain document or a permanent residence card.

Another diverse group of teens and tweens leaned over a wall and smiled in woolly hats and hazy winter sunshine.

The final text urged viewers to stay informed and directed us to the Home Office website for more information.

I felt rage bubbling up in me. Not at the content of the video in particular – I had expected it. No, it was the tone: smiling, pretty, handsome, delighted, light, fluffy, impersonal, unreal, unrepresentative. The images and the music were turning an insult into an injury. I felt patronised, undermined and angry. I shared the Home Office tweet adding: *That'll be me then. After 27 years of studying, working and paying tax here, not to mention the Scottish husband, and three kids born here. 'Rage' doesn't begin to cover it.*

Let me be clear – I generally stay out of controversy on Twitter. To be honest, I stay out of controversy in almost every aspect of my life. It was a spontaneous reaction to something which, to me, was a provocation.

I soon learned why it is wise to express no opinions on Twitter. My simple comment was shared more than 2.5k times, and more than 6.6k liked it. Many, many, many people voiced their support or sympathy. But I got my fair share of bile and abuse too. Most were subsequently removed by the platform, generally of the 'go home' variety with an imaginative range of vocabulary I choose not to say in ordinary life. Some of the more quotable ones were:

If they (foreigners) have been here that long then they should have completed the formalities long ago. Perhaps you're admitting that they're [sic] illegal immigrants. Alternatively, you're just scaremongering.

Or, *You should have sought British citizenship – simples* and *After 27 years the thought of becoming a citizen never occurred to you...* These people clearly failed to comprehend that until that point, there had simply been no need to pursue citizenship.

Other immigrants felt at least as affronted as I did:

Pure rage. Twenty years for me, Scottish partner, career, community and family. Became an adult here. My head's spinning and I feel anxious every time I think about IT. IT being, why am I being challenged in my own home?? I feel criminalised. And from another: *My father. Living, working, paying tax and NI here since 1960. 81 years old. I'm bloody livid.*

Many, many voices called for some form of civil disobedience. If enough of us didn't comply, it might break a broken system? It would raise awareness and fight the powers that be on their own turf. While this sounded romantic and attractive, it boiled down to this: I was not going to risk the wellbeing of my family. Granted, the application process for settled status was not onerous. It was a necessary evil.

The chirpy music in the promotion had offended me, yes. The thinly veiled prejudice which had become evident in some of my Twitter exchanges offended me, yes to that too. But was I going to comply? Of course I would. The risks were too great. In the wake of public outrage, the charge had been removed and applying for settled status was now free.

And so, my husband and I sat at the kitchen table by candlelight, hovering my passport over my mobile phone in the hope that the app would work, and the document would scan. I understood that in order to live in a country, I'd have to abide by its rules – it didn't mean I had to like them!

All around the UK, people like me would sit at kitchen tables like mine, hovering their own documents over their devices and hoping for the best.

* * *

If I had thought this was the end of the whole affair, I was sorely mistaken.

I pressed my phone against my ear in the kitchen and grimaced with incredulity.

'Send it away? The actual passport? To update my settled status? Are you kidding? What if I have to travel unexpectedly?'

I was incensed. I had recently obtained my new German passport after a five hour round trip to Aberdeen. Now the government was telling me I had to send the physical original, by post, to the Home Office, in the middle of a pandemic, or my settled status would cease to be valid.

'My mother is 83,' I protested weakly. 'She lives on her own in Germany. What if something happens? How long will it take before I get my passport back?'

'Around four weeks, probably,' answered the well-trained, measured voice at the other end of the phone.

What other option was there? I had to comply, didn't I? I thanked the woman politely for her time, put the receiver down and said a word I probably shouldn't.

There were so many tales of disorganisation from the Home Office. With most of the country furloughed, what were the chances of a document going missing? Against my better judgement, I wrapped my shiny new German passport in bubble wrap, shoved it in an envelope and addressed it to the EU Settlement Scheme, accompanied by a printout of the relevant online form. Resentment was still bubbling but subsiding too. *These are the new rules, this is a tough year. Don't waste your precious energy on negativity.*

I was in the middle of interviewing EU citizens for this book. Many of them felt that the only way to guarantee anything at all was to gain citizenship. Yes, there was a significant cost. But a quick inquiry to the German Consulate confirmed – as long as I applied for British citizenship before the cliff-edge at the end of 2020, I could retain my German nationality alongside gaining a British one. If I was going to do it, surely now was the time.

Finding a lawyer to navigate the process was tricky. Time was running out. Would it be worth trying on my own? I was a graduate! Surely, I'd be able to navigate a Home Office online application.

In any case, the first step was to book a Life in the UK test. Given that by then I had lived in the UK for 29 years, it felt a little insulting, but rules were rules. I fed my details into the Home Office website. Available slots in Belfast and Newcastle were comedy options, given that I lived in Inverness, in lockdown. I kept scrolling. Nothing in Edinburgh for at least two months. Eventually, I spotted a single slot in Glasgow. Click!

It was mine. A quick online payment, and let the revising begin!

My local Waterstones bookseller knew me well through author events, NessBookFest and my regular purchases. He stared wide-eyed. 'You have to apply?' he asked as he scanned the shiny £12.99, 2020 edition of the *Life in the UK Test Study Guide* for me. 'I can't believe they don't just give it to you automatically after all these years. It's not like you've contributed anything to this country, huh?'

A little voice in me agreed with his last sarcastic remark. Having him and so many others in my corner felt like a virtual hug in socially distanced times.

As I walked home through leafy October streets, I tried to rationalise it all. This was my favourite month of my favourite season in my least favourite year – the yo-yo of Covid restrictions and their easing was taking its toll on everyone I knew. Rob's job as a Public Health doctor had changed beyond all recognition. Let's call it what it is: a small thing in a sea of big things. I was not going to let this get to me. Highlighter in hand, I began to read.

The whole thing seemed more like a narrow-minded ill-thought-out game of Trivial Pursuit in which you're on your own:

Which of the following statements is correct?
- Mary Peters won gold at the 1976 Olympics in the 200 metres
- Mary Peters became team manager for the women's British Olympic team

What?
I had no idea!
Nor did I know the name of the historic piece of legislation which gave every prisoner the right to a court hearing, or the registration systems for voters in different parts of the UK. I knew nothing about youth court procedures, or the location of the National Horseracing Museum; wasn't sure whether the Royal Society is the oldest scientific organisation in the world, how independent Chief Constables are and who or what Clarice Cliff is. How many national parks are there in England, Wales and Scotland combined? What did the reform acts of 1832 and 1867 do? Who sat on the British throne at the time of the Bayeux Tapestry?

Oh my word, this was going to be harder than I thought. The thing that rankled the most was that I was certain that most Brits of my acquaintance, many of whom are very educated, wouldn't know the answers either.

Meanwhile, headlines about the dying moments of Brexit talks dominated the media:

Boris Johnson still refusing to restart Brexit negotiations despite ticking no-deal clock

Brexit news – live: France tells Boris Johnson 'no new approach' from EU, as Brussels warns time running out

Brexit: EU citizens in UK could be shut out of vital services. Fears that shift from paper to digital permits could prevent those with settled status accessing jobs, banking and healthcare

A fortnight later, I made the rainy journey to Glasgow. Three-and-a-half hours by car. Half an hour to find the building and park up. Forty-five minutes in the test. Waiting for the result. A quick, socially distanced catch-up with our oldest who is studying at the University of Glasgow and the three-and-a-half-hour return journey. All of this was sandwiched in a week of interviews with some of the artists, scientists, academics and public servants who are featured in these pages.

* * *

I wish I could offer a satisfying and tidy ending to this book, worthy of a story. As an author of fiction for children, storytelling is what I do. But this is no simple story; it is a saga, generation after generation, person after person, crisis after crisis.

By the time you read this, the Brexit referendum result will be half a decade old. I will have lived and worked in Scotland for 30 years. I may have gained British citizenship, or I may not. All around me, immigrants like me will arrive and leave. Perhaps the cooking pot of Europe will stir a little less as a result of recent events.

But I maintain, through all of this, that the sum of all the ingredients is what makes the dish appealing.

By limiting ourselves to one, we only risk dulling our senses.

Postscript

WHY WRITE THIS book at all?

I suppose people have a right to ask. I, as an incomer, claim a place on Scottish bookshelves as a children's writer. My books are mostly historical fiction set in Scotland. Shouldn't there be disclaimer somewhere? *This author is foreign, just so you know.*

What right does an immigrant have to tell the story of a land that is not her own? I myself have wrestled with these questions over the decades. It's all about identity: the identities I claim for myself, the identities bestowed on me by others, and the value we place on these. Belonging, it turns out, can be a choice.

The immigrant voice matters. It is my lived experience, and the many interviews with EU nationals included in these pages only attest to the fact that there are many stories, like mine and unlike mine, which have become part of the warp and weft of Scottish society. Like threads, some shine brightly. Others are almost invisible but lend the tapestry its stability.

As an incomer to Scotland, I am immensely grateful for the hospitality, warmth and encouragement I have received, from people born in Scotland and those born elsewhere. All of them are part of the warp and weft of my own life. They have formed my thinking, honed my skills, fired my imagination, put food on my table. Their threads shine brightly.

But do I not have the right to comment on the society I have inhabited for three decades? Am I not entitled to make the case, based on my own experience, for open-minded exchange with other cultures and ideas? We have left the European Union. That is done. However, in the ensuing discourse we are in danger of losing something valuable, swept away in a current of nostalgia and propaganda which would have us 'return' to a Britain that never really existed.

As my *Scottish by Inclination* project nears its end, in the midst of a pandemic, and with my citizenship application still in progress, I choose hope.

As all crises do, this crisis will pass. Many Scots, and many, many Brits, are tolerant, welcoming and curious about the world.

Myself, and all the EU citizens featured in this book have chosen to belong. We are Scottish by Inclination.

And we are going to be okay.

Acknowledgements

MY FIRST THANKS must go to all those Europeans who have kindly agreed to let me feature their stories in Scottish by Inclination. I am immensely humbled by the trust you have put in me, and I hope I have done it justice.

Thanks to Gavin MacDougall for spotting the potential in the idea for the book, for honing the vision and for pointing me towards funding. I gratefully acknowledge support from the National Lottery through Creative Scotland towards the writing of this title.

My thanks also to all at Luath Press: Carrie for her editorial insight and expert cover design, Jennie for expert typesetting and endless patience in long phone calls, Lauren for publicity wizardry and Eilidh for expert production – it certainly takes a village to create a book!

Thank you to the writers, academics and reviewers who have taken the time to read *Scottish by Inclination* and seen fit to endorse it. As my first attempt at non-fiction and memoir, your encouragement has meant the world. I am also grateful to Robert Davidson for his enthusiasm – without it I may not have believed in the project myself. Thank you.

But above all, thanks to Rob for allowing me to tell my story (which is also his) and to Carla, Isla and Duncan. You're my pack. I may have come to Scotland as an immigrant, but you have made it home. I am utterly blessed to call you mine.

Luath Press Limited

committed to publishing well written books worth reading

LUATH PRESS takes its name from Robert Burns, whose little collie Luath (*Gael.*, swift or nimble) tripped up Jean Armour at a wedding and gave him the chance to speak to the woman who was to be his wife and the abiding love of his life. Burns called one of the 'Twa Dogs' Luath after Cuchullin's hunting dog in Ossian's *Fingal*. Luath Press was established in 1981 in the heart of Burns country, and is now based a few steps up the road from Burns' first lodgings on Edinburgh's Royal Mile. Luath offers you distinctive writing with a hint of unexpected pleasures.

Most bookshops in the UK, the US, Canada, Australia, New Zealand and parts of Europe, either carry our books in stock or can order them for you. To order direct from us, please send a £sterling cheque, postal order, international money order or your credit card details (number, address of cardholder and expiry date) to us at the address below. Please add post and packing as follows: UK – £1.00 per delivery address; overseas surface mail – £2.50 per delivery address; overseas airmail – £3.50 for the first book to each delivery address, plus £1.00 for each additional book by airmail to the same address. If your order is a gift, we will happily enclose your card or message at no extra charge.

Luath Press Limited
543/2 Castlehill
The Royal Mile
Edinburgh EH1 2ND
Scotland
Telephone: +44 (0)131 225 4326 (24 hours)
Email: sales@luath.co.uk
Website: www.luath.co.uk